Sheila Bird is amongst the best known of contemporary writers on Cornwall, and is also known for her work as a broadcaster on Radio Cornwall. She is the author of *The Book of Cornish Villages* (Dovecote Press, 1988), *Around the Waterways of the Fal*, as well as books on bygone Falmouth, Penzance and Newlyn, and Truro. She has travelled throughout the county in search of the curiosities in this book, and has visited all of them.

Frontispiece
The Lander Column, Truro (see No. 36)

Cornish Curiosities

Sheila Bird

Photographs by Oriel Hicks

THE DOVECOTE PRESS

To Philip Hennessy, with thanks

First published in 1989 by The Dovecote Press Ltd
Stanbridge, Wimborne, Dorset BH21 4JD

ISBN 0 946159 69 6

© Sheila Bird 1989

Photoset in Times by Character Graphics, Taunton, Somerset
Printed and bound by Biddles Ltd
Guildford and King's Lynn

Contents

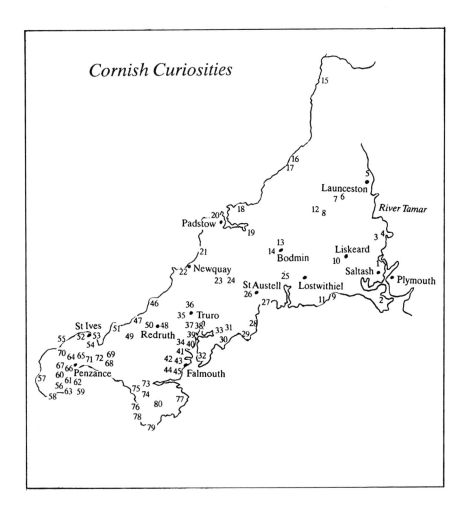

Cornish Curiosities

15

16
17

Launceston
7 6

5

12 8

River Tamar

18

20

Padstow

19

3 4

13

Liskeard

14 Bodmin

10

21

Saltash

Plymouth

22 Newquay

25

23 24

St Austell

Lostwithiel

26

46

27

36

11 9

2

35 Truro

47

St Ives 51

50 48

37 38

28

55 52 53

49 Redruth

33 31

29

54

39

30

34 40

41

70 64 65 71 72 69

42 43 32

67 66 68

44 45 Falmouth

57 60

56 61 62

73

58 63 59

75 74

76 80 77

78

79

8

Introduction

A guide book written earlier this century declared enthusiastically that 'to visit Cornwall is to travel beyond the bounds of the commonplace'. Today's travellers from across the Tamar, looking at the strange Celtic names on the signposts, and venturing into the green and grey Cornish landscape, with its moorlands, hills, flower strewn hedgerows, deep wooded combes, picturesque rivers, wide estuaries, and bordered by the longest coastline in Britain, soon become aware of this. In Cornwall, where dreams and reality seem to merge, nature has created a landscape of curiosities. Within that landscape, early man left intriguing imprints, and successive generations of Cornish folk have implanted functional, work-a-day structures, connected with their struggle for survival, which appear to us today as quaint and pleasing. Many are a source of wonder, particularly when we learn why and how they came to be there, and give some insight into the ingenuity and indefatigability of the Cornish race. How many of our modern structures will survive the test of time as functional and pleasing?

In Cornwall, where truth is so often stranger than fiction, and usually more interesting, there is no need to colour reality with oft repeated legends. So in compiling this book, I have veered towards an informative, practical approach to curiosities in the landscape, with themes and cross references. In selecting the curiosities I have aimed at variety and originality, representing the whole county, and have chosen those with visual impact, and which can be visited or easily observed.

In compiling this book I should like to acknowledge the help of many individuals, particularly Terry Knight, Joanne Hillman and Kim Springall of the Local Studies Library, Redruth, and to the Harbour Master, Deputy Harbour Master at Mevagissey and Henry Johns. Thanks also to Falmouth Library, the Private Lending Library, Morrab Gardens, Penzance, the Royal Institution of Cornwall, Truro, Plymouth Tourist Information Centre, Goonhilly Satellite Earth Station, Delabole Slate Quarry, English China Clays, English Heritage, the National Trust, Falmouth Maritime Museum, the Potter Museum of Curiosity and Museums at Looe, Bodmin, Penryn and Mevagissey.

1 Brunel's 'Triumphal Arch' into Cornwall

Position: Royal Albert Bridge across the Tamar, Saltash
Ordnance Map: Plymouth & Launceston: Sheet 201 1:50 000
Map Ref: SX/432/587
Access: The best way to view the bridge is from a Tamar river steamer, or from a train. It can also be seen to good effect from the shores of Saltash, Torpoint, Plymouth, or points upstream.

Note: The opening of the Royal Albert Bridge in May 1859, described as a 'triumphal arch' into Cornwall, was a turning point in Cornish history, providing a railroad link with mainstream Britain. *The West Briton* was in awe of Isambard Kingdom Brunel's proposed project: 'Fancy, then, these two enormous arches built on the top of a pier nearly twice as high as Truro spire; and then imagine railroad carriages dashing on at railroad pace over this terrific structure!'

Great crowds came to witness the more spectacular stages of its development, particularly the sinking of the two diving bells, and the ceremonial opening by Prince Albert. When asked how long he envisaged his bridge being there, Brunel replied, 'A hundred years; explaining it would no longer be needed after that time. Sadly he was close to death, and he died a few weeks after being drawn across his masterpiece in a specially adapted truck. His prediction was wrong; a century later this double spanned wonder was joined by the modern suspension bridge, crossing the estuary in one mighty (1100 feet) span.

Places of Interest in the Neighbourhood
2. Whimsical, Ruined and Bizarre
4. All in Clover
9. Looe's 'Quaint and Ancient Pile'

2 Whimsical, Ruined and Bizarre

Position: Maker Folly at Mount Edgcumbe, to the west of Plymouth
Sound
Ordnance Map: Plymouth & Launceston: Sheet 201 1:50 000
Map Ref: SX/457/524
Access: From Cornwall follow A38 to Trerulefoot roundabout, then
the A374 and the B3247 to Crafthole, Millbrook & Mount Edgcumbe.
From Plymouth by Cremyll Ferry for pedestrians. Vehicles via
Torpoint ferry, follow A374 to Antony, then B3247 to Mount
Edgcumbe.

Note: After their move to Mount Edgcumbe from Cotehele in the 16th
century, the Edgcumbe family built the mansion that bears their name.
It occupies a hilly promontory jutting into the sea to the west of
Plymouth harbour, and looks out over the Sound.

By the 18th century, when the aristocracy were creating classical
gardens with lakes, temples, statues and fountains, many adorned their
estates with a romantic ruin. Thus the folly at Mount Edgcumbe was
conceived and constructed in 1747, as a genuine, purpose built artificial
ruin. Some of the stone may have come from an obelisk which once
stood on the site, and the doorways and windows of two medieval
chapels at Stonehouse on the Plymouth shore may have been used.

Mystery surrounds the virtual disappearance of that old obelisk, and
the appearance of another one near Cremyll, outside the estate, which
strangely bears no inscription. It seems that an eccentric 18th century
Countess of Mount Edgcumbe favoured a pet pig as a constant
companion, even calling it Cupid. The story goes that she was so
distraught when it died that she raised the anonymous obelisk in its
memory. This bizarre relationship was the inspiration for an ode by the
18th century satirist, Peter Pindar (John Wolcot).

Ode To The Countess Of Mount Edgcumbe
On The Death Of Her Pet Pig Cupid

Oh! dry those tears so round and big,
Nor waste in sighs your precious wind,
Death only takes a little pig.
Your Lord and son are still behind!

Places of Interest in the Neighbourhood
1. Brunel's 'Triumphal Arch' into Cornwall
4. All in Clover
9. Looe's 'Quaint and Ancient Pile'

The Maker Folly, Mount Edgcumbe

3 The Turnpike Cottage

Position: The Tollgate, Callington, between the junction of Saltash
Road and the secondary road to St Germans
Ordnance Map: Plymouth & Launceston: Sheet 201 1:50 000
Map Ref: SX/361/693

Note: The gabled building with unusual decorative embellishments to
its gables, windows, chimneys and corners, was originally constructed
as a turnpike house. The Turnpike Trusts were established in Cornwall
by Act of Parliament, and the money put forward for these schemes
and subsequent road maintenance was recouped by means of tolls. The
payments were widely resented – and avoided – and there was
jubilation in 1874 when it was announced that the Callington Turnpike
Trust was to be wound up, for it was said that Callington was nine miles

from everywhere, with turnpike gates studded around the town like so many forts around a castle. They were likened to 'impassable barriers, which seem to say to every rider on horseback and to the driver of every vehicle . . .from the fishmonger and regrator, to the merchant and the esquire "so far shalt thou go and no farther – without paying!"

This obsolete turnpike cottage, once the scene of such animation, was forgotten until James Chubb, proprietor of the Temperance Hotel in Well Street (later to become Callington Social Club), bought the property and embellished it in order to attract travellers and well heeled townsfolk. A large dining hall was built earlier in the century, where local farmers jovially met on market days, and it became a venue for social groups as well as commercial travellers and holidaymakers. Indeed, it became more of a way of life than a family run business, with staff and visitors who had returned year after year visiting Miss Mabel Chubb in her home after her retirement, a few years ago. Today part of it is divided up into flats, while the area created by the Chubbs is a wine bar and restaurant, and remains a local venue.

Places of Interest in the Neighbourhood
 1. Brunel's 'Triumphal Arch' into Cornwall
 2. Whimsical, Ruined and Bizarre
 4. All in Clover
 5. Execution and Penal Servitude at Launceston Castle
 6. 'One of the most Endearing Monuments in Cornwall'
10. Measures of Mineral and Liquid Plenty

4 All In Clover

Position: The restored barge *Shamrock*, on display at Cotehole
Quay(NT) on the west side of the Tamar
Ordnance Map: Plymouth & Launceston: Sheet 201 1:50 000
Map Ref: SX/423/681

Note: The sailing barge *Shamrock* on display at Cotehele Quay is an
example of the specially designed shallow draught vessels built for the
tidal creeks and small harbours of Devon and Cornwall. She was
constructed by Frederick Hawke at Stonehouse, Plymouth in 1899. In
the 1950s she was a familiar sight around Falmouth and the waterways,
where she was able to get in on the tide ahead of her rivals and carried
roadstone from the coastal quarries at Porthoustock, on the Lizard, to
the depot at the Tresillian. After being involved with salvage work and
left to rot in the creek off Plymouth harbour, *Shamrock* was rescued
and renovated at Cotehele Quay and restored to her appearance of
1926, under the supervision of Tom Perkins and the National Maritime
Museum.

Cotehele Quay, with its attractive 18th and 19th century buildings,
evokes those glorious days of waterborne-trade. In the middle of the
last century the facilities here and at Bohetherick collectively provided
seven limekilns, a large granary, coal stores, timber yards, salt stores
and yards for the storing of mineral ores and manure. At Cotehele
there was also a public house, brewery and malt house, stables and
labourers' cottages. In the heyday of the river, these quays played a
significant role in the local mining, brick, lime and quarrying
industries, ships returning up-river with much needed coal, ironware and
limestone.

Cotehele House, originally built around 1485, was the first of the
Edgcumbes' houses and contains original furniture, armour and
needlework. There are lovely gardens, a medieval dovecote and a
restored mill.

Places of Interest in the Neighbourhood
 1. Brunel's 'Triumphal Arch' into Cornwall
 2. Whimsical, Ruined and Bizarre
 3. The Turnpike Cottage
 6. 'One of the most Endearing Monuments in Cornwall'
10. Measures of Mineral and Liquid Plenty

5 Execution and Penal Servitude at Launceston Castle

Position: Launceston Castle at the summit of Dunheved Hill, Launceston
Ordnance Map: Plymouth & Launceston: Sheet 201 1:50 000
Map Ref: SX/327/845

Note: Launceston, described by the poet Charles Causley, one of its most famous sons, as 'a distinctive frontier town', has long been dominated by its castle, commandingly situated on Dunheved Hill. After the Norman Conquest a wooden palisade and tower were constructed with protective earthworks, and it became the principal seat from which Cornwall was governed. By the beginning of the 13th century, the timber had been replaced by stonework, with an added tower, moat and buildings within curtain walls.

Despite its indominitable appearance, it was stormed four times during the Civil War, after which it suffered neglect and by the end of the 18th century was being used to house prisoners and foraging pigs. In 1820, when Bodmin Gaol became full, the prisoners sentenced to hard labour were transferred to Launceston Gaol, and the Mayor, Richard Penwarden came up with the practical solution of setting the prisoners to tidy up the mound, even issuing them with extra beer.

Such men were the more fortunate. This is where Cuthbert Mayne, who was seized at Golden Farm near Grampound for ministering Catholicism to leading families at a time of religious suppression in the 16th century, was hanged, drawn and quartered (see No. 19) and where the Quaker pioneer George Fox and so many others suffered over the centuries.

Places of Interest in the Neighbourhood
  3. The Turnpike Cottage
  4. All in Clover
  6. 'One of the most Endearing Monuments in Cornwall'
  7. From Obscurity to Fame ... and back Again
  8. 'A Far Famed Mere'
  10. Measures of Mineral and Liquid Plenty
  12. A Museum of Curiosities

6 'One of the most Endearing Monuments in Cornwall'

Position: Inside North Hill Church, North Hill
Ordnance Map: Plymouth & Launceston: Sheet 201 1:50 000
Map Ref: SX/272/767

Note: The importance of Cornwall's leading families can be gauged by their ancestral memorials in the county's churches. This impressive collection of sculptured memorials described by Nikolaus Pevsner as 'one of the most endearing monuments in Cornwall', and which

undoubtedly influenced the sculptor Nevil Burnard as a young boy (see No 7) can be savoured all the more for being in such a remote and beautiful part of the county. The Spoure monument of 1688, with its realistically coloured figures, depicts Henry Spoure kneeling with his wife, while two children are positioned in niches behind them. The Spoures occupied Trebartha, which came to them in the late 15th century, when the heiress Anna Trebartha married one of Henry VIII's captains, who had been sent to Cornwall to quell a rebellion. It passed to the Rodd family after another heiress, Mary, left it to her fiancé in 1729. The house, which was pulled down just after the last war has left its name to the tiny hamlet to the north-west of North Hill.

Another impressive memorial in this church, in slate and dating from the early 17th century, depicts Thomas Vincent of Batten and his wife, along with their seven daughters and eight sons. A tombstone to Arthur Peter in the churchyard is the work of the young Burnard.

Places of Interest in the Neighbourhood
3. The Turnpike Cottage
5. Execution and Penal Servitude at Launceston Castle
7. From Obscurity to Fame . . . and back Again
8. 'A Far Famed Mere'
10. Measures of Mineral and Liquid Plenty

7 From Obscurity to Fame . . . and back Again

Position: Plaque on birthplace of Nevil Northey Burnard in Altarnun, just north of the A30 between Launceston and Bodmin
Ordnance Map: Plymouth & Launceston: Sheet 201 1:50 000
Map Ref: SX/224/813

Note: The circular slate plaque on the wall of the cottage adjacent to the former Wesleyan Meeting House, recalls that this was the birthplace in 1818 of Nevil Northey Burnard, the self taught Cornish lad who became a fashionable portrait sculptor in London. The relief portrait of John Wesley in blue grey Polyphant stone above the chapel doorway is one of the many examples of his early work to be found scattered widely around the county.

The son of a stonemason, he found that slate, sometimes referred to as 'Cornish marble', offered the ideal medium. His designs were influenced by the flora and fauna of the surrounding countryside, and the traditional motifs he had seen in the local churches, particularly at nearby North Hill.

Exhibiting his work at the Polytechnic Society in Falmouth led to its President, Sir Charles Lemon of Carclew introducing him to London's most eminent sculptor, Sir Francis Chantry. During those thirty years in London, he went from strength to strength, fashioning the features

of the famous on the 19th century literary, artistic, scientific, religious and political scene. He was also a welcome guest at Penjerrick House, near Falmouth, home of the Fox family. Some might argue that his later style, studied and stereotyped, lacked the freshness and vitality of his early Cornish work.

And then tragedy struck. His eleven year old daughter Lottie died in 1870. Grief-stricken and in despair he returned to Cornwall to wander the roads as a vagrant, dying in Redruth Workhouse in November 1878. The man who had sculpted so many memorials to others was himself buried in an unmarked pauper's grave in Camborne churchyard. But seventy six years later Camborne Old Cornwall Society erected a simply inscribed Delabole slate tombstone to this previously little acknowledged Cornish genius whilst the poet Charles Causley was instrumental in having a tablet placed on his birthplace in 1968.

Places of Interest in the Neighbourhood

8 'A Far Famed Mere'

Position: Dozmary Pool, on Bodmin Moor, to the south of Bolventor
Ordnance Map: Plymouth & Launceston: Sheet 201 1:50 000
Map Ref: SX/193/746
Access: By the winding lane off the A30, opposite Jamaica Inn

Note: Dozmary Pool is an isolated bogland lake lying on high, open moorland, amid an array of hut circles and other prehistoric remains, and it must rate as one of the county's strangest natural curiosities. Not surprisingly, it has long attracted myth and legend. For centuries country folk believed that a tide here 'did ebb and flow', that the waters were deep, even bottomless, and that there was a whirlpool in the middle. Furthermore it was linked with John Tregeagle, that infamous Cornish bogeyman who sold his soul to the Devil, and was doomed to bail these waters with a leaking limpet shell for eternity. Legend also has it that Sir Bevidere reluctantly cast the magical sword Excalibur into these waters, at the bidding of the dying King Arthur, and that a hand and arm clad in white samite emerged from the water to catch it and draw it back down beneath the surface.

Another watery tale, but decidedly more chilling, concerns an acre of ice one foot thick, whisked away daily for some fishy purpose. But this one was true; there *was* an ice factory here in the last century, with reservoirs and storage houses for the storage of compressed ice, to supply the fisheries of Newlyn.

Places of Interest in the Neighbourhood
6. 'One of the most Endearing Monuments in Cornwall'
7. From Obscurity to Fame . . . and back Again
10. Measures of Mineral and Liquid Plenty
12. A Museum of Curiosities

9 Looe's 'Quaint and Ancient Pile'

Position: Old Guildhall, Higher Market Street, East Looe
Ordnance Map: Plymouth & Launceston: Sheet 201 1:50 000
Map Ref: SX/255/534

Note: East Looe's Old Guildhall, described in an early guidebook as a
'quaint and ancient pile' is thought to have been built around 1500,
initially as a single storey structure, with an upper floor being added to
provide a council chamber and courthouse as befitted the town after
receiving its charter from Queen Elizabeth in 1587. A covered stairway
and porch give access to the council chamber, with attractive
woodwork. Set within the gable is an old pillory, which either catered
for two heads and two hands, or had two appertures removed to align
the useful piece of timber for its new role. Some of Looe's inhabitants
of sixty years ago recall the pillory carrying out its primary function.
The main feature of the building was the magistrates' raised deck
reached by a short flight of steps on each side, with an old Royal Arms
frescoed above it, while in former times a staircase just below the
Bench led down to the cells. The one time Council and Justice Hall
later became a public newspaper room; restored in 1972 it now
functions as a museum within a museum. The stocks, which once stood
outside on the cobbles along with the pillory, have been preserved as
has a picture of the old Ducking Stool.

As Looe expanded during the latter part of the last century, the Old
Guildhall, like Looe's lovely old bridge, was seen as obsolete, and
replaced by a new Guildhall. Ironically, disenfranchisement of the
Borough in 1886 left the inhabitants with two Guildhalls – but no
Borough.

Places of Interest in the Neighbourhood
 1. Brunel's 'Triumphal Arch' into Cornwall
 2. Whimsical, Ruined and Bizarre
 4. All in Clover
10. Measures of Mineral and Liquid Plenty
11. Picturesque and Pleasing

10 Measures of Mineral and Liquid Plenty

Position: Fine old buildings in The Parade, Liskeard & Pipe Well, in
Well Lane
Ordnance Map: Plymouth & Launceston: Sheet 201 1:50 000
Map Ref: SX/252/646

Note: Liskeard owes its prosperity to the copper ore from the granite
from the Cheesewring quarries. Its prestige is reflected in its fine
buildings, particularly those around The Parade, including the Town
Hall, the Market Hall and Webb's Hotel, as well as various 'copper
money' Regency houses.

The name *Fountain Inn* traditionally symbolised the liquid plenty
contained in the coopers' casks, and here it combined these hoped for
liquid assets with the well or fountain down the lane, which has never
been known to run dry. It was here that Dr Taylor, 'the well known
water doctor from Manchester', 'respectfully' made it known in 1816
that he would be available for consultations, inviting his patients to
bring along early morning samples of their urine to determine whether
they were curable or not. Alternatively ailing folk could try their luck
at the nearby Pipe Well, formerly known as the Well of Lyskiret or the
Well of St Martin, whose waters were thought to have 'lucky effects in
matrimony' as well as qualities of healing. Possibly as a result of over
enthusiasm for the former, the original well was sealed off and the four
iron pipes we see today, connected to the springs in Victorian times,
gave rise to the present name.

Places of Interest in the Neighbourhood
3. The Turnpike Cottage
6. 'One of the most Endearing Monuments in Cornwall'
9. Looe's 'Quaint and Ancient Pile'

11 Picturesque and Pleasing

Position: The harbourside area of Polperro
Ordnance Map: Plymouth & Launceston: Sheet 201 1:50 000
Map Ref: SX/208/510

Note: Polperro is one of Cornwall's classic fishing villages. Its quaint
and tightly wedged colour washed cottages climb and cling to the steep
hillsides overlooking the picturesque harbour. It is best visited out of
season, when one can relish the apparently whimsical, but essentially
work-a-day style of architecture. The intriguing *House on Props*, built
on supports above the water, may look merely picturesque, but it is
perched there to be safely above the flood level. But the house in the
Warren encrusted with shell designs, ships, lighthouses, towers,
circles, stars, diamonds, squares, butterflies, flowers, is decorated just
for the fun of it.

  The changes of placename, originally a Porth (meaning cove) and
now a Pol (meaning pool), and variously known as Portpira,
Porthpera, Porthpire, Porth Pyre , Polperra, Polparrow and now
Polperro, puzzles the experts. But its colloquial name of Polstink is less
of a mystery.

Places of Interest in the Neighbourhood
 9. Looe's 'Quaint and Ancient Pile'
10. Measures of Mineral and Liquid Plenty

Potter's Museum of Curiosity, Jamaica Inn

12 A Museum of Curiosities

Position: Potter's Museum of Curiosity, in an annexe of Jamaica Inn, Bolventor, on the right hand side of the A30, when travelling westwards, between Launceston and Bodmin
Ordnance Map: Plymouth & Launceston: Sheet 201 1:50 000
Map Ref: SX/183/768

Note: An isolated old coaching hostelry in the middle of Bodmin Moor seems an unlikely place to come across a splendid array of Victorian curiosities, where stuffed animal exhibits are set amidst a colourful background, as if frozen from some favourite childhood storybook, and where tooth, fang, fur, feather and claw live in perfect harmony.

Walter Potter, born in Sussex in 1835, worked in his father's inn and stuffed animals as a hobby. One day his sister showed him a nursery rhyme book and the illustration of 'The Death And Burial Of Cock Robin' gave him the idea of bringing them together as an illustrative group in a romantic setting, in a style the Victorians took to their hearts. The commissions rolled in, enabling him to become a full time taxidermist whose creations graced many a parlour.

The most famous Cornish coaching hostelry, Jamaica Inn, is romantically situated in the heart of the wild and rolling Bodmin Moor at Bolventor, and became immortalised in Daphne du Maurier's novel of the same name. But how did a remote, moorland inn come by such an exotic name? For centuries it was known as the New Inn, but the name was changed in honour of one of the Rodd family of local squires, who had held a post in Jamaica, and returned to Cornwall to end his days in the much loved haunts of his childhood.

Places of Interest in the Neighbourhood
7. From Obscurity to Fame . . . and back Again
8. 'A Far Famed Mere'

13 Fulfilling the Promise of his Name

Position: The Gilbert Obelisk, Beacon Hill, to the south east of
Bodmin
Ordnance Map: Newquay & Bodmin: Sheet 200 1:50 000
Map Ref: SX/067/664

Note: The prominently positioned 144 feet high obelisk, designed by
Thomas Eva of Helston which dominates the approach to Bodmin,
honours Walter Raleigh Gilbert, who was born in Helston in 1785 and
moved to Bodmin at an early age.

He was to fulfil the patriotic promise of his name but on land rather
than sea. He joined the British Army, served in India rose to the rank
of Lt General and was created a baronet. A large number of Cornish
relatives and friends attended his London funeral in 1853, while in his
home town the shops closed as a mark of respect, and the minute bell
tolled dolefully from noon till one.

It is particularly fitting that his memorial was erected on The
Beacon, close to the old wrestling ring, for this had been the area where
local folk had long enjoyed the delights of the Bodmin Riding. And it
was he who was instrumental in getting the Bodmin Races re-
established here in 1833. He was never happier than when astride a
horse.

Places of Interest in the Neighbourhood
14. A Teacher on the Treadmill
19. The Bridge Built on Wool
24. A Natural Phenomenon for Elevated Thinking
25. A Reminder of 'The King of mid Cornwall'
27. Charlestown; a Visionary's Dream

14 A Teacher on the Treadmill

Position: Bodmin Gaol, Berrycombe Road, Bodmin (0208 76292)
Dungeons & Museum open to the public 10-6.00, Easter-mid October
(not Saturdays)
Ordnance Map: Newquay & Bodmin: Sheet 200 1:50 000
Map Ref: SX/072/672

Note: When the county gaol at Launceston fell into decay, an Act of
Parliament in 1778 allowed for the construction of a new one in
Bodmin, which came into use about a year later. Built under the
auspices of Sir John Call, J.P., an eminent military engineer, on the
principles of humane prison reformer John Howard, it was a
prestigious undertaking, thought to be ahead of its time, and described
in 1873 as being 'one of the most perfect in the West of England.'

Part of its down to earth philosophy was to segregate hard offenders,
lesser criminals who might be reformed, debtors and women; to isolate
prisoners at night and position cells away from outer walls. The inmates
were encouraged to use their time creatively, producing saleable items
to raise money for their deprived families. Furthermore, in 1838, when
most of the inmates were found to be illiterate, one of the inmates was
employed to take reading and writing classes with the men and boys.
This arrangement worked well until the teacher was removed for
misconduct, and placed on the treadmill. In the absence of another
suitable candidate from within, the school was suspended, with the
chaplain earnestly advocating an unfettered replacement.

Part of the prison was rebuilt in 1855, and in 1888 the sections of the
building previously used for debtors and women became a Royal Naval
prison. Today Bodmin Gaol is open to the public.

Places of Interest in the Neighbourhood
13. Fulfilling the Promise of his Name
19. The Bridge Built on Wool
24. A Natural Phenomenon for Elevated Thinking
25. A Reminder of 'The King of mid Cornwall
27. Charlestown; a Visionary's Dream

15 An Array of Potty Chimneys

Position: The former vicarage by Morwenstow Church, Morwenstow, north of Stratton.

Ordnance Map: Bude & Clovelly: Sheet 190 1:50 000

Map Ref: SS/205/153

Access: Look for signs, from the A39, to the north of Kilkhampton.

Note: Just below Morwenstow's ancient church, whose graveyard is the last resting place of many a shipwrecked victim, is a substantial looking house, formerly the vicarage of the Rev Robert Stephen Hawker, poet, mystic and notable eccentric. The building is dominated by an array of strange looking chimneys, projecting somewhat heavily heavenwards, representing church and college towers with which he had associations, and a likeness of his mother's tomb. But perhaps this whimsical incongruity is a fitting reminder of the cleric who created a home of this 'manse in ruins', brought dignity to victims of shipwreck in death, and devoted 40 years of his life to the service of 'a mixed multitude of smugglers, wreckers and dissenters,' and who delighted in attracting attention by being flamboyant and outrageous. This much loved but controversial man had inscribed on a slab of slate above his porch:

> A House, A Glebe, A Pound a Day,
> A pleasant Place to Watch and pray;
> Be true to Church, Be Kind to Poor,
> O Minister, For evermore.

Hawker's first wife was twice his age, his second young enough to be his grand-daughter. He also wrote, and it is said that the hut now known as Hawker's Hut, from ships' timbers hauled up from the beach, was built as an inspirational studio. Furthermore this is reputedly where his friend Alfred Tennyson wrote the haunting poem 'Break, Break, Break . . .' capturing the sadness of a young fisherman's death.

Hawker has found a permanent place in Cornish history for his Trelawny ballad, adopted as the Cornish National Anthem. Initially he published it anonymously, apparently with the intention of deceiving people into thinking it was a genuine 17th century song, written when one of the Trelawny family was committed to the Tower by James II, thereby becoming a popular folk hero.

Places of Interest in the Neighbourhood
5. Execution and Penal Servitude at Launceston Castle

16 A 14th Century Architectural Gem

Position: The Old Post Office, Tintagel
Ordnance Map: Newquay & Bodmin: Sheet 200 1:50 000
Map Ref: SX/056/884

Note: This quaint and sturdy slate built 14th century manor house, incorporating a large hall, remains as a tribute to those early craftsmen who worked sympathetically with local materials to create an architectural gem. As needs arose, the original building was extended, with extra chimneys, stairs and gables adding their pleasing proportions to the overall effect. For more than half of the last century this building was used as a post office, and was saved from possible demolition in 1895 by Miss Johns, who bought the property at auction. It is now in the care of the National Trust, and open to visitors during the season.

Places of Interest in the Neighbourhood

17 The Largest Hole in Britain

Position: The Slate Quarry, Pengelly, Delabole
Ordnance Map: Newquay & Bodmin Sheet 200 1:50 000
Map Ref: SX/073/838
Access: Take the turning to Pengelly off the B3314, in Delabole village

Note: Delabole Slate Quarry, with its vital statistics embracing a
circumference of a mile and a half and a depth of 500 feet, is reckoned
to qualify as the largest man made hole in Britain. Furthermore its
name Delabole, derived from the 13th century Delyou Bol, meaning
'Deli with a pit,' is an indication of the number of centuries it has taken
generations of Cornishmen to dig this big hole.

As a metamorphic stone, quarried from the Devonian rocks, this
blue grey close textured Delabole slate is renowned for its endurance
and high quality. It was used in roofing and flooring most of the houses
and churches in Cornwall, and its everyday familiarity led to it being
nicknamed 'Cornish marble.'

Traditionally the slates were split into standard sizes, attractively
known as Ladies, Countesses, Duchesses, Queens and Imperials,
which possibly added a slightly feminine touch to the rough and tough
world of the quarriers.

There has been a recent revival in the Delabole Slate Quarrying
industry, for real slate is back in demand for top quality roofing, as well
as facing, flooring and ornamental functional features, including
fireplaces. The quarry is not open to the public, but a viewing area and
showroom provide the opportunity to marvel at the largest man made
hole in Britain.

Places of Interest in the Neighbourhood
16. A 14th Century Architectural Gem
19. The Bridge Built on Wool
20. Padstow's Notorious Doom Bar

18 Narrowly Entering *The Guinness Book of Records*

Position: The Narrow Streets of Port Isaac, and The Bird Cage
Ordnance Map: Newquay & Bodmin: Sheet 200 1:50 000
Map Ref: SX/996/808

Note: This picturesque old fishing port, with its white painted, slate
hung cottages hugging the steeply sided combe of the enclosed bay and
harbour, is one of the least spoilt in Cornwall, thanks to its hilly
situation and exceptionally narrow streets. Fore Street is only seven
feet wide. The colloquially named Squeeze Belly Alley, measuring just
19½ inches across, is the narrowest of a number of such alleyways or
drangs in Port Isaac, thereby gaining the distinction of being
mentioned in *The Guinness Book of Records*. Visitors are intrigued by
The Bird Cage, an asymmetrical building just above the harbour,
which was constructed as a fisherman's cottage, neatly filling the space
available at the time. When the settlement was first established, trade
and communications were primarily by water, and so the emphasis was
on the harbour and the day to day needs of the fishermen and their
boats.

   In the last century it was also traditional for thanksgiving services for
the harvest of the sea to be held in Port Isaac church, suitably
decorated with fish, flags, flowers, pots, nets and other fishing tackle.

Places of Interest in the Neighbourhood
16. A 14th Century Architectural Gem
17. The Largest Hole in Britain
19. The Bridge Built on Wool
20. Padstow's Notorious Doom Bar

19 The Bridge Built on Wool

Position: The bridge over the Camel at Wadebridge
Ordnance Map: Newquay & Bodmin: Sheet 200 1:50 000
Map Ref: SX/991/723

Note: It was Thomas Lovibond, vicar of Egloshayle, concerned about
the dangers of crossing the ford over the tidal River Camel at
Wadebridge, who was responsible for the construction of the 17 arched
bridge in the 15th century. The money derived, mostly on taxes from
wool, gave rise to the expression 'a bridge built on wool,' which some
interpreted literally as meaning physically constructed on woolsacks.
This myth is commemorated by the inn here, called The Bridge On
Wool. The bridge differed from other Cornish bridges in that it was
built on endowed land, managed by a band of feoffees. It became a
county bridge during the reign of James I, and was kept in repair partly
from the revenue derived from estates, and partly by tolls.

The bridge has borne sad witness to cruel happenings. The gentle
and learned priest Cuthbert Mayne, who was captured at Golden
Farm, near Grampound, and hanged in 1577 at Launceston (see No 5),
was quartered, with parts of his body put on display at various sites,
including the middle of the bridge.

This fine old bridge, the longest in Cornwall and one of the best
examples of a medieval bridge in Britain, was widened in 1847 and
1962.

Places of Interest in the Neighbourhood

20 Padstow's Notorious Doom Bar

Position: Doom Bar, at the Camel estuary, about 1½ miles to the north of the port of Padstow
Ordnance Map: Newquay & Bodmin: Sheet 200 1:50 000
Map Ref: SX/917/777
Access: Doom Bar can be seen from the Padstow or Trebetherick shores, where there is a good network of footpaths offering beautiful views of the whole estuary.

Note: Holidaymakers may rejoice at Padstow's vast expanse of gleaming sands, but the apparently benign and sheltered estuary of the Camel is notorious in the annals of our seafaring history. The wide entrance of the haven, bordered by Pentire Head to the north and Stepper Point to the south, conceals an unexpected hazard a mile or so within its embrace, in the form of a sandbank running out from the eastern shore, which has been the doom of many a coastal schooner, smack, brigantine, barque, sloop, trawler, small steamer and its hapless crew. This was also the scene of major lifeboat disasters in 1865 and 1900. Although Doom Bar may sound like a tailor made name for this fateful bank of sand, it was anciently known as Dun Bar.

The Camel haven was always important to shipping, particularly in the days of sail, as it was the only estuary on the north coast, apart from Hayle, in which vessels could seek shelter in stormy conditions. The lighthouse on Trevose Head, to the west of the Camel estuary, was constructed in 1847, after a disastrous series of shipwrecks along the coast, re-affirming the oft quoted rhyme:

> From Padstow Point to Lundy Light,
> Is a sailor's grave by day or night.

Places of Interest in the Neighbourhood
18. Narrowly Entering *The Guinness Book of Records*
19. The Bridge Built on Wool
21. Stacks and Steps and Good Queen Bess
22. The 'Hevva! Hevva!' House
23. Queen's Pit

21 Stacks and Steps and Good Queen Bess

Position: On the coast, about 6 miles to the north of Newquay on the B3276
Ordnance Map: Newquay & Bodmin: Sheet 200 1:50 000
Map Ref: SX/848/695

Note: For centuries the Atlantic has pounded these dramatic shores, creating at Bedruthan Steps picturesque erosion in the form of stacks, steps or islets along the sandy coastline, backed by perpendicular cliffs. The stacks can be seen best from the beach at low tide, particularly at the northern end, when a striking likeness to Good Queen Bess emerges in full profile. The largest of the stacks is known as Diggory Island, near Pentire.

Bedruthan Steps, now a steep cliff staircase by which it is possible to reach the beach in summer, was originally a series of zigzag cuttings in the cliff face, which some people say was for the convenience of wreckers and smugglers. The romantically inclined would cite the so called Parson's Prayer: 'Lord! We do not pray for wrecks, but since there must be some, grant we beseech Thee, that they may be on our beach.' This was where the brigantine *Samaritan* was driven ashore in 1846 in a gale, with the loss of five crew. If the well known rhyme is to be credited, the local reaction completely contradicted the Biblical significance of the brigantine's name:

> The Good Samaritan came ashore
> To feed the hungry and clothe the poor,
> Barrels of beef and bales of linen . . .
> No poor man shall want a shillin'.

These steps were once the only access to the shore. Then around 1849 an easier path was excavated from the rock face, to which the name Bedruthan Steps was transferred. These became undermined by erosion, and partly subsided during a storm. They have since been refashioned, and today this favourite beauty spot can be savoured from the top by those unable to tackle the steps, where there is a National Trust shop, information centre, cafe and facilities.

Places of Interest in the Neighbourhood
19. The Bridge Built on Wool
20. Padstow's Notorious Doom Bar
22. The 'Hevva! Hevva!' House
23. Queen's Pit
46. 'The Cornish Wonder'

22 The 'Hevva! Hevva!' House

Position: Huers' Hut on Towan Head, Newquay
Ordnance Map: Newquay & Bodmin: Sheet 200 1:50 000
Map Ref: SX/805/624

Note: Although the pleasing clifftop Huers' House, with its squat tower, diamond shaped windows and rudimentary castellations possesses the charm of a folly, it was a functional, work-a-day look-out post from which the huers watched for approaching pilchard shoals. When the tell-tale signs were spotted on the surface of the water, the air resounded with the cries of 'Hevva! Hevva!' (A shoal! A shoal!). Whereupon fishing crews took to their seines, while the huer on the clifftop directed operations either by shouting through a hailer, or by signalling with a furze bush or whitened canvas covered hoops. There would be three or four boats to each great net. Stop nets were employed to block the mouths of the seines, and tuck nets used to empty out the haul.

In early times part of the catch was sold on the shore; the remainder was bulked and pressed. The salted fish was packed into barrels and exported, mostly to the Mediterranean countries. The oil was used to fuel lamps, while the unsaleable fish and used salt was sold as a fertiliser. Nothing was wasted.

The work of the huer demanded skill, as this advertisement of 1848 testified: 'Wanted, for a Pilchard Sean, at Newquay a steady intelligent man as huer, and an active man, with some decision about him as master seaner. None need apply but those who have had much experience in Pilchard Fishing.'

Places of Interest in the Neighbourhood
21. Stacks and Steps and Good Queen Bess
23. Queen's Pit
46. 'The Cornish Wonder'

23 Queen's Pit

Position: Indian Queens, on the A30 between Redruth and Bodmin
Ordnance Map: Newquay & Bodmin: Sheet 200 1:50 000
Map Ref: SX/918/587
Access: Travelling westwards on the A30, look for Pocohontas
Crescent, on the left, just beyond the Port And Starboard Cafe in the
village of Indian Queens

Note: Mining activity, which had been going on for centuries in this
area of Goss Moor, reached a peak in the 18th century, when the
preacher John Wesley passed this way after drawing congregations of
Biblical proportions at the impressive and legendary Gwennap Pit.

   Just a couple of hundred yards away from the bustle of the A30 lies
an unexpected haven of peace. This stepped, rounded amphitheatre,
an unexpected jewel in the Indian Queens' crown, is Queen's Pit,
thought to have been inspired by Gwennap, and similarly fashioned
from an old mine working; in this case adapted from Wheal Fatwork tin
mine.

   If this constitutes a metaphorical jewel in the Queen's crown, who
was the queen who lent her name to the village? The village took its
name from an inn whose sign bore a picture of Queen Victoria's head
on one side and a Red Indian on the other. Queen Victoria was often
depicted as Queen of the Empire (including India), hence Queen (or
Empress) of India. To add to the confusion, an inscription about a
Portuguese princess is said to have been carved on the lintel of the inn's
doorway, but the pub has been demolished and no one knows what

happened to the lintel. Portuguese? Indian? Red Indian? Princess or Queen?

The favoured theory is that the name recalls Pocohontas, the Red Indian princess, who fell in love with Captain John Smith, founder of Virginia. Legend relates that she came to England with her second husband, John Rolfe in 1616, when her Plymouth bound ship was diverted to Falmouth because of bad weather, and that she stayed here overnight, on route for London. She is buried at Gravesend.

Places of Interest in the Neighbourhood
22. The 'Hevva! Hevva!' House
24. A Natural Phenomenon for Elevated Thinking
26. The Secret of a Chinese Mountain which transformed a Cornish Landscape

Roche Rock, Roche

24 A Natural Phenomenon for Elevated Thinking

Position: Roche Rock, at Roche, to the north of St Austell, on the B3274
Ordnance Map: Newquay & Bodmin: Sheet 200 1:50 000
Map Ref: SX/596/991

Note: The northern edge of St Austell's china clay mining area is well known for its rocks, which are outliers of the Hensbarrow Beacon. The most striking and famous of these is a tough quartz schorl outcrop at Roche, capped by the ruined chapel of St Michael. A guidebook of 1824 tells us that 'A ride to the Roche Rocks, which are situated almost six miles from Bodmin, will be highly gratifying for the curious traveller, or an admirer of natural curiosities. They consist of three immense piles of craggy, ponderous stones, rising to a considerable height, and at a distance resembling an ancient castle.' Dr Richard Pococke, travelling through the county in 1750, wrote of the famous rock with its hermitage, which was ascendable by a precarious ladder, adding 'even some ladies of masculine courage have gone up into it.'

Predictably, this impressive stone has attracted colourful stories concerning that favourite Cornish bogeyman Tregeagle. Attempting to pay penance after selling his soul to the Devil, Tregeagle disturbed the resident hermit. Some stories tell of this being the refuge of a shunned leper, whose dutiful daughter brought him daily water from the now vanished well.

Places of Interest in the Neighbourhood
13. Fulfilling the Promise of his Name
14. A Teacher on the Treadmill
23. Queen's Pit
25. A Reminder of 'The King of mid Cornwall'
26. The Secret of a Chinese Mountain which transformed a Cornish Landscape

25 A Reminder of 'The King of mid Cornwall'

Position: The Treffry Viaduct, Luxulyan
Ordnance Map: Newquay & Bodmin: Sheet 200 1:50 000
Map Ref: SX/058/568
Access: Take the secondary road northwards to Luxulyan from the A390 near the railway crossing at St Blazey.

Note: This beautiful granite viaduct carrying a diverted stream and railroad over the lovely Luxulyan valley was described in 1874 as 'the finest piece of masonry in all Cornwall'. It was built between 1825 and 1830 by Joseph Thomas Treffry, a public-spirited magnate and mining adventurer, who gained the prestigious nickname of 'the King of mid Cornwall.'

This much admired structure, 700 feet long and nearly 100 feet high, with its ten graceful arches, carried not only Treffry's copper from Fowey consuls mine to Newquay to be exported to South Wales for smelting, but also gave rise to new china clay workings by opening up a line to the port of Par, where the terrain had proved difficult for horse-drawn waggons. Treffry's vision transformed the decaying port of Par, and it has since kept abreast of today's fast changing technology in the exporting of china clay.

Places of Interest in the Neighbourhood
13. Fulfilling the Promise of his Name
14. A Teacher on the Treadmill
23. Queen's Pit
24. A Natural Phenomenon for Elevated Thinking
26. The Secret of a Chinese Mountain which transformed a Cornish Landscape

26 The Secret of a Chinese Mountain which transformed a Cornish Landscape

Position: Conical China Clay Tips, viewed from Penwithick, on the
B3374 between St Austell and Bugle
Ordnance Map: Newquay & Bodmin: Sheet 200 1:50 000
Map Ref: SX/024/555

Note: During the 18th century a large section of the Cornish landscape,
particularly on the high moors above St Austell, was totally
transformed as the result of a Chinese puzzle being worked out by a
Plymouth apothecary. For the well guarded secret of producing finest
quality pottery, known as porcelain, had originated on the Chinese
mountain of Kao Lin, where the potential of the mineral which came to
be known as kaolin or china clay was first exploited. The secret reached
Saxony, where a porcelain factory was established in the 18th century,
arousing the curiosity of William Cookworthy, a Plymouth apothecary.
After obtaining samples Cookworthy realised that china clay was
produced by the decomposition of granite and feldspar, which led him
to the discovery of china clay at Tregonning Hill near Helston in 1745.
In 1768 he took out his patent for the manufacture of porcelain. The
Midland potters, although interested in setting up factories, found it
more viable to move the clay where coal and the needs of industry were
more readily available, than to found factories in Cornwall. By 1840 all
the potters had relinquished their leases, and pits were being worked
by local Cornish families.

For the St Austell district, where the recession in the tin, copper and
iron mines had forced hundreds of miners to emigrate, this was a timely
opportunity for the workers to apply their relative skills in an emerging
new industry. Cornwall can be proud that the county today 'houses the
World's largest producer of China Clay, English China Clays P.L.C.'

Wheal Martyn, the China Clay museum, situated 2 miles north of St
Austell on the A391, is open from the beginning of April to the end of
October and gives a fascinating insight into the story of china clay.

Places of Interest in the Neighbourhood
24. A Natural Phenomenon for Elevated Thinking
27. Charlestown; a Visionary's Dream
28. Mevagissey's Old Watch-house
29. Grandeur and grim Romanticism

27 Charlestown; a Visionary's Dream

Position: Charlestown, to the south east of St Austell
Ordnance Map: Newquay & Bodmin: Sheet 200 1:50 000
Truro, Falmouth & surrounding area: Landranger 204 1:50 000
Map Ref: SX/037/517

Note: Following the discovery of china clay in the St Austell area in the late 18th century, large amounts of clay were shipped to the Midlands for the production of porcelain. Most of the cost of the pottery could be attributed to expensive and inefficient transportation until Charles Rashleigh, a local squire and mining speculator, saw ways of overcoming the delays and dangers caused by ships beaching on the foreshore to load and unload in the time honoured way.

He approached John Smeaton, the engineer responsible for building the Eddystone lighthouse and St Ives Pier, to design a purpose-built port at Polmear for the handling of china clay. The pier was started in 1791, and a basin excavated from the rock to accommodate vessels of up to 400 tons and a draught of 15 feet. Lock gates and wharves were constructed and the port renamed Charlestown in honour of Squire Rashleigh of Menabilly (1747-1825).

China clay has always been the principal commodity handled here, but as empty ships represent loss of potential wealth, they returned with coal, coke, timber, iron and limestone. So in order to avoid off-white china clay and dusty grey coal they separated these working areas, which gave rise to two 'breeds' of Charlestown workers; those covered in white dust, and their more sombre counterparts. Hence this delightful mid-19th century traveller's description: 'At first we could see nothing, but gradually our eyes accustomed themselves to the murk, and we made out that on one side of the harbour vessels were being loaded with china clay, and their crews were white as millers. On the other side coal was being discharged, and the crews were as black as Erebus. The villagers were black or white according to which side of the port they resided on, while some were both black and white like magpies.'

Charlestown's Shipwreck And Heritage Museum has some interesting exhibits concerning life here in days gone by, in addition to well as well displayed items concerned with diving and shipwrecks.

Places of Interest in the Neighbourhood
25. A Reminder of 'The King of mid Cornwall'
28. Mevagissey's Old Watch-house
29. Grandeur and grim Romanticism

28 Mevagissey's Old Watch-house

Position: Old Watch-house, on the quay at Mevagissey
Ordnance Map: Truro, Falmouth & surrounding area:
Sheet 204 1:50 000
Map Ref: SX/016/448

Note: The distinctive old Watch-house, which is so much a part of
Mevagissey, was originally built for the coastguards and revenue men.
An interesting photograph of 1875 shows the bow-windowed watch-
house, with its conspicuous flagpole before the outer harbour was
built, while photographs of 1890 show these smartly uniformed officers
by the open doors beneath that bow window, from which their cutter
could be rapidly launched down the slipway. The Top House addition
dates from 1925.

One 19th century preventive officer boarded a vessel off Chapel
Point and left it without finding any contraband only to later notice a
sudden light from her which was answered by another. He arrested the
two Mevagissey fishermen despite their protests that they were merely
lighting up their pipes.

The attractive building, used by generations of harbour masters,
caught the imagination of film makers in 1944, when it featured in the
swashbuckling *Johnny Frenchman*, and references to this and other
aspects of Mevagissey's history can be seen at the adjacent museum.

Places of Interest in the Neighbourhood
26. The Secret of a Chinese Mountain which transformed a Cornish
    Landscape
27. Charlestown; a Visionary's Dream
29. Grandeur and grim Romanticism
30. Keeping the Devil at Bay
31. Who Stole the Clockworks?

29 Grandeur and grim Romanticism

Position: The Dodman to the south west of Gorran Haven
Ordnance Map: Truro, Falmouth & surrounding area Landranger 204
1:50 000
Map Ref: SX/002/393
Access: It can be approached by steep, narrow lanes from Gorran
Haven or via Boswinger. The best way to get there is by using the
coastal footpath.

Note: The Dodman, that dark, forbidding, gorse clad headland,
capped by an Iron Age promontory fort and Bronze Age barrows, and
scene of many a harrowing shipwreck, must be the grandest headland
on Cornwall's southern coast. But despite its earlier name of
Deadman, with apparent connotations of shipwreck and tragedy, the
name was more likely a corruption of the earlier Dudman, from the
family who farmed for the landowning Bodrugans. An alternative
theory suggests a Scandinavian/Celtic derivation, denoting a bold
headland, but originally it went by the somewhat tamer name of
Penare; a name which survives in the adjacent farm.

Whatever the derivation of its name, the headland has long been a
well-loved landmark for returning seafarers, immortalised in sea
shanties, and commanding magnificient views. In 1896, a former rector
of Caerhayes, who had a special love of the spot had a sturdy granite
cross erected on the seaward summit, inscribed with the words, 'In the
firm hope of the second coming of our Lord Jesus Christ, and for the
encouragement of those who strive to serve.' Shortly afterwards this
was the scene of a naval disaster. For in conditions of thick fog *HMS
Lynx* and *HMS Thrasher*, destroyers from Devonport, struck, the
Dodman's rocky extremity, instantly killing three sailors and fatally
injuring two more as a steam pipe was fractured. The extensively
damaged vessels were released on the flood tide.

Places of Interest in the Neighbourhood
26. The Secret of a Chinese Mountain which transformed a Cornish
    Landscape
28. Mevagissey's Old Watch-house
30. Keeping the Devil at Bay
31. Who Stole the Clockworks?

30 Keeping the Devil at Bay

Position: The Round Houses at Veryan, on the Roseland Peninsula, to
the south of Tregony
Ordnance Map: Truro, Falmouth & surrounding area Sheet 204 1:50 000
Map Ref: SW/917/396

Note: It was whimsically said that Veryan's delightful thatched and
whitewashed round houses, with their conical roofs surmounted by
crosses, were constructed with no north side for the Devil to enter, and
no dark corners where he might lurk. The crosses on the top added a
third means of keeping him at bay. Some would also point out that they
were built at the ends of the village, so that if the Devil came prowling,
he would encircle the protected round houses, and never be able to
enter the village and would finally retreat to leave Veryan in peace.

These curious circular cottages constructed of cob, with oddly
shaped and decorated windows and doors, were built in the last
century. Although each is unique, they collectively conform to a quaint
and pleasing general pattern.

Places of Interest in the Neighbourhood

31 Who Stole the Clockworks?

Position: Tregony Clocktower, in Tregony's main street
Ordnance Map: Truro, Falmouth & surrounding area Sheet 204 1:50 000
Map Ref: SW/926/450

Note: Tregony, a medieval port on the once navigable upper reaches of the River Fal was a Roseland marketing centre and early Borough, disenfranchised as a Rotten Borough in 1832. At the upper end of the main street stands a pleasing looking town clock tower, with a heavy studded door at its base.

When the clock was built as a memorial to Richard Gurney, a rector and magistrate at the time of the disenfranchisement, it was assumed by some to belong to the Corporation, and by others to have been presented to the inhabitants. So when Dr Jewel started selling off Corporation property around 1856, John Dunstone of Tregony, who purchased the town hall, fair park and market house assumed that the clocktower was thrown in as a job lot. It was his intention to send it to Australia. Just before Christmas in 1861, the inhabitants of Tregony were outraged when it was found that someone had carried out an early morning raid on the turret, and carried off the clock's weights and pendulum. Eventually the official winder up of the Town Clock appeared and took possession of the clock, the bells, the dials and the vane, and carted them away to the cheers of an enthusiastic crowd, leaving the once proud clocktower in a sorry state. Confusion surrounds the rest of the tale, for it seems that Dunstone was offered £12 as some form of compensation, and the clock then mysteriously re-appeared.

The clocktower was restored in 1864, and the original clock replaced by a striking clock with two hands in 1928. The tower now bears the additional inscription: E II R 1952-1977.

Places of Interest in the Neighbourhood
28. Mevagissey's Old Watch-house
29. Grandeur and grim Romanticism
30. Keeping the Devil at Bay
33. The Ruined Quay
35. The Cornish Giant in a Prestigious Institution
36. With Classical Lemon Street at his Feet

32 Built to Defend, but swift to Surrender

Position: St Mawes Castle, at the entrance to Falmouth Haven, St
Mawes [English Heritage]
Ordnance Map: Truro, Falmouth & surrounding area Sheet 204 1:50 000
Map Ref: SW/841/320
Access: To St Mawes by road from the Roseland side, or by ferry from
Falmouth

Note: St Mawes and Pendennis Castles, the twin sentinels at the
entrance to Falmouth haven, were built between 1540 and 1546 as part
of Henry VIII's coastal defensive scheme, but each reacted differently
in the face of strife. St Mawes castle, low and squat, was built with a
central tower and three lower bastions, creating a complex of defensive
circles calculated to deflect cannon balls yet offering the widest
possible field of fire from within. Captained by successive members of
the Vyvyan family, who stood for the King at the time of the Civil War,
St Mawes castle surrendered immediately to a landward attack, while
Pendennis, under the elderly Colonel John Arundel stuck out for a six
month siege.

   During the middle of the last century improvements were made to
the castle, and ordnance brought in. Wise captains of passing ships
gave it wide berth when local coastguards used it for firing practice.
Later in the century, when the place was manned by two Royal
Artillery gunners from Pendennis, it was thought scandalous that their
weekly pay should be specially brought across in a garrison boat with
six men and a coxswain, when it could have been delivered at a trifle of
the cost.

Places of Interest in the Neighbourhood
30. Keeping the Devil at Bay
33. The Ruined Quay

33 The Ruined Quay

Position: The ruined quay at Ruan Lanihorne, to the south west of
Tregony
Ordnance Map: Truro, Falmouth & surrounding area Sheet 204 1:50 000
Map Ref: SW/888/419
Access: From Ruan churchtown, take the low road westwards towards
Sett Bridge, and look for traces of the ruined quay and bollards by the
unfenced roadside on the left.

Note: A plaque set into the decaying quay at Ruan Lanihorne tells us
that the quay and foreshore was presented to the parish in 1919. This is
a reminder that until comparatively recent times, trade and
communications around these parts were mainly by water. When the
silting up process, accentuated by the indiscriminate dumping of waste
mining material upstream strangled the ancient port of Tregony (See
No. 31), Ruan Lanihorne became the head of navigation.

In the 18th century there were quays and warehouses, and it was
recorded that ships of 80 to 100 tons docked with coal and timber, and
barges brought sand. During the 19th century the Martyn brothers of
Ruan leased a coalyard, malthouse and quay. Rather surprisingly,
ochre, mined for a short time at Veryan, arrived in horse drawn carts to
be taken by barge up to Truro and shipped to London. Back in the
1920s, local folk from the outlying rural areas came here in horse drawn
traps on Wednesdays and Saturdays for the trip up to Truro aboard the
steam launch *Amy*. But today the silting up has made such pleasures
impossible.

Places of Interest in the Neighbourhood
30. Keeping the Devil at Bay
31. Who Stole the Clockworks?
32. Built to Defend, but swift to Surrender
35. The Cornish Giant in a Prestigious Institution
36. With Classical Lemon Street at his Feet

34 'Timber!' and 'Tally Ho!'

Position: The Norway Inn, Perranarworthal on the A39 between Truro and Falmouth
Ordnance Map: Truro, Falmouth & surrounding area:
Sheet 204 1:50 000
Map Ref: SW/778/386

Note: The sign of the Norway Inn close to the water at Perranarworthal is a local reminder of the colourful days of trade by water, when great baulks of Norwegian timber for the Gwennap mines and Perran Foundry was brought into Restronguet Pool and rafted up this creek at high water.

Despite its altered appearance, this evocatively named old hostelry also recalls the coaching era. The prestigious Post Office Packet Service from Falmouth (see No. 42) required the best of overland communication links with Exeter and London. Thus in 1754 a short turnpike was constructed from Falmouth to Truro and Grampound. Toll cottages were built along the turnpikes, with a clear view of traffic from both directions (see No. 3).

The first stage appeared on the scene around 1790, running on

alternate days from Exeter to Falmouth, via Bodmin, and taking around 21 hours to cover 100 miles. A variety of vehicles soon evolved, including horse omnibuses, daily waggons, vans, long coaches, stage waggons and the somewhat lumbering 'flying waggons'. The Exeter and Falmouth Quicksilver Mail created a fine spectacle racing along the turnpike roads 'like fire racing along a trail of gunpowder'; their guards decked out in red and gold livery. In 1859 the Quicksilver coach, which left Falmouth at 11 a.m., changed horses at the Norway Inn, then called at the Royal Hotel, Truro, the Falmouth Arms, Ladock, Indian Queens on Goss Moor, the Royal Hotel at Bodmin, and Jamaica Inn at Bolventor (see no. 12), before arriving at Launceston that evening.

Places of Interest in the Neighbourhood
35. The Cornish Giant in a Prestigious Institution
36. With Classical Lemon Street at his Feet
37. The Come-to-Good Meeting House
38. Echoes of Rapunzel?
39. Feock's Detached Church Tower
40. The former Royal Naval Dockyard
41. A 17th Century Fire Engine

35 The Cornish Giant in a Prestigious Institution

Position: Full length portrait of Anthony Payne in The Royal Institution of Cornwall, River Street, Truro (Truro Museum)
Ordnance Map: Truro, Falmouth & surrounding area Landranger 204 1:50 000
Map Ref: SW/823/448

Note: Anthony Payne, sometimes referred to as 'the Falstaff of the West,' or known to one and all as The Cornish Giant, is depicted in the R.I.C.'s full length painting of 1680 by the court artist Sir Godfrey Kneller wearing his uniform as Halberdier of the guns of Plymouth Citadel.

Stories surrounding this towering mountain of a man have grown with time. He was born in the manor house at Stratton, now known as the Tree Inn, and some say that when he died a big hole had to be bored in the ceiling to get his body downstairs. References to his size became absorbed into the language; hence the expression 'as long as Tony Payne's foot!' And then there is that old rhyme about his sword:

> His sword was made to match his size,
> As Roundheads did remember;
> And when it swung 'twas like the whirl
> Of windmills in September.

The Royal Institution of Cornwall, Truro

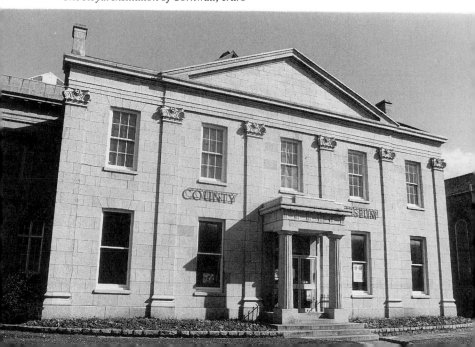

He was an asset in anyone's army, and he fought beside Sir Bevil Grenville at the Battle of Stamford Hill in 1643.

The Royal Institution of Cornwall's classical building and its proud traditions merit attention in their own right, and are unique. This institution was established in 1818 for the promotion of knowledge in natural history, archaeology, ethnology and the fine arts, as well as for the encouragement of literature. Although Truro was already enjoying recognition as a cultural centre, it was a bold move. Originally known as the Cornwall Literary And Philosophical Society, it became known as the Royal Institution of Cornwall after George IV gave it his patronage. These River Street premises were opened by the Prince of Wales in 1919, and have recently been extended.

Places of Interest in the Neighbourhood
36. With Classical Lemon Street at his Feet
37. The Come-to-Good Meeting House
38. Echoes of Rapunzel?
39. Feock's Detached Church Tower

Anthony Payne, The Cornish Giant
(courtesy of The Royal Institution of Cornwall, County Museum)

36 With Classical Lemon Street at his Feet

Position: The Richard Lander Column, at the top of Lemon Street, Truro
Ordnance Map: Truro & Falmouth: Sheet 204 1:50 000
Map Ref: SW/824/445

Note: The impressive, fluted Doric column, at the top of Truro's Lemon Street, surmounted by a statue of the explorer Richard Lander, harmonising with the classicism of its pleasing surroundings, also pays tribute to his brother John, the deaf and dumb architect Philip Sambell, who designed the column, and Nevil Northey Burnard who sculpted the likeness (see No. 7).

The statue depicts Lander with his head inclined towards the observer, which is more personal than the usual aloof gaze, dressed in loose trousers and a frock coat. The design as a whole incorporates the spirit of the River Niger, with water motifs, foliage, native animals as well as the explorer's tropical kit. The palm branch in his hand symbolised his travelling in peace, but in fact this African explorer was to die violently in a native ambush. The inscription honours 'the enterprise and sufferings of the brothers Richard and John Lander, natives of this town, and especially to commemorate the early fate of Richard, explorer of the River Niger, born 1804, died Fernando Po 1834.'

Places of Interest in the Neighbourhood
35. The Cornish Giant in a Prestigious Institution
37. The Come-to-Good Meeting House
38. Echoes of Rapunzel?
39. Feock's Detached Church Tower

37 The Come-to-Good Meeting House

Position: Quaker Meeting House. Come-to-Good, near Feock, to the
east of the A39 between Truro and Falmouth
Ordnance Map: Truro, Falmouth & surrounding area:
Sheet 204 1:50 000
Map Ref: SW/814/403

Note: The thatched and whitewashed Quaker Meeting House, situated
in the pleasingly named hamlet of Come-to-Good (*Cwm ty coit*, the
coombe by the dwelling in the wood') is a fine example of early 18th
century domestic architecture, impressive in its simplicity and with an
air of rare tranquillity. It was built to a rectangular design in 1710, of
cob construction beneath an open timbered, thatched roof, but it was
subequently extended, and stabling was provided for the worshippers'
horses. A 'loft' supported by two wooden pillars was added in 1717. It
was accessible by a steep staircase, up which the children were allowed
to 'creep very quietly.'

Come-to-Good was formerly close to the ferry crossing on an old
route through Cornwall; a highway traversed by traders and pilgrims in
early times. During the 17th century the pioneering Quakers were
cruelly persecuted and often imprisoned for their faith. The
descendants of George Fox, who was thus cast into Launceston Gaol,
were later to establish themselves in the Falmouth area, where they
continue to prosper.

Today Come-to-Good is a much cherished Meeting house for local
Friends and others, for whom it is a place of pilgrimage.

Places of Interest in the Neighbourhood
34. 'Timber!' And 'Tally Ho!'
38. Echoes of Rapunzel?
39. Feock's Detached Church Tower
40. The former Royal Naval Dockyard
41. A 17th Century Fire Engine

38 Echoes of Rapunzel?

Position: Trelissick Tower, to the right of the B3289 at Trelissick, just west of the King Harry Ferry
Ordnance Map: Truro & Falmouth: Landranger 204 1:50 000
Map Ref: SW/836/396
Access: Can be viewed from the roadside or from Trelissick Gardens (NT)

Note: Trelissick House, reckoned to be the finest Palladian mansion in Cornwall, is surrounded by enchanting gardens sweeping down to the River Fal, with open views down Carrick Roads and of ships laid up in King Harry Reach. In a setting of such romanticism, the whimsical looking round tower capped by a weather vane of a bushy tailed squirrel cracking a nut, might well be mistaken for a folly. Could this be where Rapunzel let down her hair? In fact it is a purpose built Water Tower, constructed around 1860, and now converted for use as a holiday cottage.

Places of Interest in the Neighbourhood
37. The Come-to-Good Meeting House
39. Feock's Detached Church Tower
40. The former Royal Naval Dockyard
41. A 17th Century Fire Engine

39 Feock's Detached Church Tower

Position: Detached church tower in the centre of Feock village
Ordnance Map: Truro, Falmouth & surrounding area: Sheet 204 1:50
000
Map Ref: SW/825/384
Access: To the south east of the A39 Truro to Falmouth road, turning
off at Playing Place and following the signposts

Note: The detached tower on the slope above the mainly 19th century
church of St Feoca is virtually all that remains of that original 13th
century building. It is one storeyed, with a pyramidal roof, and some
say it was erected to create a lookout down the section of River Fal
known as Carrick Roads, and thereby a landmark. It contains three
bells, thought to have been cast from a larger, medieval one. These still
chime for services. This church was reputedly where the last service in
the Cornish language was held.

The war memorial later placed beside the tower is a reminder of the
incredible number of youngsters who went to war and never returned.
A walk around the churchyard recalls the Ferris, Ford and Hitchens
families of boatbuilders, and the fine tradition of boatbuilding around
the river and creeks.

Places of Interest in the Neighbourhood
37. The Come-to-Good Meeting House
38. Echoes of Rapunzel?
40. The former Royal Naval Dockyard
41. A 17th Century Fire Engine

40 The former Royal Naval Dockyard

Position: Mylor Yacht Harbour, Mylor Churchtown
Ordnance Map: Truro, Falmouth & surrounding area: Sheet 204 1:50 000
Map Ref: SW/819/354

Note: The Western Approaches and Cornwall's southern waters were
the scenes of many a skirmish during the 18th and 19th centuries, when
our ships were subject to attack by enemy vessels, privateers and
pirates, so Falmouth haven was an obvious place of refuge. The
potential of the natural deep water anchorage off Mylor, with the
advantage of not being too obvious from the sea, had been documented
by the King's topographer John Leland in 1533. The area now known
as Mylor Yacht Harbour was excavated from the swampy shores at the
beginning of the 19th century to create a Royal Naval Dockyard and,

The Ukranian Monument, Mylor

by 1805, work was progressing on a pier, stone wharf, cooperage and storage sheds. The project included a reservoir, boathouse, masthouse, iron house, pitch house, smithy and slipway as well as sail and other stores and accommodation for officers.

After the Post Office Packet Service was taken over by the Admiralty in time of war (see No. 42) *HMS Astraea* was anchored offshore to serve as a storeship. Old naval brigs which took over the role of transporting the mails came here for re-coppering and repairs instead of having to return to Plymouth. But the safety record of these vessels, which tended to fall victim to their own decay, earned them the unfortunate nickname of 'coffin brigs'. The overcrowding of Falmouth's graveyards resulted in the Admiralty acquiring a section of Mylor churchyard for burial of those who died aboard their ships in the harbour.

The churchyard is the last resting place for many victims of shipwreck. Particularly poignant are the Transport *Queen* grave and the monument to the orphan boys of the Training Ship *HMS Ganges*, who experienced incredible hardship and deprivation in their short lives. Between Mylor Bridge and Restronguet Barton is a monument of thanksgiving, erected by Ukrainians, who found refuge here after escaping from Russian Communists in the Second World War. Some of them remained here, married and brought up families.

Places of Interest in the Neighbourhood

41 A 17th Century Fire Engine

Position: Exhibited inside Penryn Exhibition Hall in Penryn's Town
Hall, on an island in the centre of the main street
Ordnance Map: Truro, Falmouth & surrounding area: Sheet 204 1:50 000
Map Ref: SW/783/345

Note: A sturdy, wooden 17th century mobile fire fighting appliance
stands inside Penryn's Town Hall, looking rather like an outsize
favourite toy. Basically it is a water container on four solid wheels,
topped by a pumping handle and bellows, with inlet and outlet pipes,
both gravity fed. Along the two sides run leathern hoses with metal
studs, in remarkably good condition, which fitted into the pipes. A 19th
century fire engine on display nearby is similarly cart-like, but with
spoked wheels, and ladders carried aloft.

Places of Interest in the Neighbourhood
40. The former Royal Naval Dockyard
42. Saluting the Men of Falmouth's Post Office Packet Service
43. 'A Beauty to the Harbour without Limitation of Time . . .'
44. The King's Pipe
45. Four Bunks for Five

The Packet Service Monument, Falmouth

42 Saluting the Men of Falmouth's Post Office Packet Service

Position: Monument to the men of the Packet Service in the centre of
The Moor, Falmouth
Ordnance Map: Truro, Falmouth & surrounding area: Sheet 204 1:50 000
Map Ref: SW/806/328

Note: The monument in the centre of Falmouth's now busy area known
as The Moor, reclaimed from the marsh, and thronging with cars, taxis
and buses, is a tribute to the men of the Post Office Packet Service,
whose daily lives called for courage and fortitude.

Falmouth became the headquarters of the Post Office Packet Service
in 1688, initially to Corunna, Lisbon, then to the West Indies and parts
of North America. This extended to Nova Scotia, Mexico, Brazil and
Argentina after 1706. These little vessels, often carrying gold bullion
and valuable cargoes, attracted the attentions of Algerian pirates,
French, Spanish and American privateers and French men o' war.
During the Napoleonic Wars they were frequently engaged in
skirmishes, with the odds stacked heavily against them. As mail
carriers, albeit armed, they were under strict orders to fight only if
attacked, and if cornered, to sink the mails and surrender. During the
18th century naval vessels carried out reconnaissance work and
protected convoys. The Admiralty took over the Packet Service in
1823, replacing the packet ships with small sloops of war. Many of
these armed brigs, deep waisted, low decked and in poor shape, fell
victim to attack or their own lack of seaworthiness. Their penchant for
disappearing without trace, together with their unfortunate
passengers, cargoes and mails, earned them the grim nickname of
'coffin brigs.' In the 19th century it was quite common to see the little
packet ships heaving their homeward way past Pendennis Point, under
clouds of canvas. 'And often, too often there would be sighted,
staggering across the bay, a battered hull with shattered masts and
spars, torn sails and dismantled guns, as a little Post Office boat, having
sunk or beaten off her enemy, crawled laboriously home.'

Places of Interest in the Neighbourhood
41. A 17th Century Fire Engine
43. 'A Beauty to the Harbour without Limitation of Time . . .'
44. The King's Pipe
45. Four Bunks for Five

43 'A Beauty to the Harbour without Limitation of Time . . .

Position: Killigrew Monument: Grove Place (between Arwenack
Street & Bar Road) Falmouth
Ordnance Map: Truro, Falmouth & surrounding area: Landranger 204
1:50 000
Map Ref: SW/812/325

Note: The granite pyramid in Grove Place recalls the enterprising but
piratical Killigrew family, who built Arwenack House (now restored

and converted after years as a ruin) in the late 16th century, when this was a tiny fishing settlement known as Smithwick. They saw its potential, not only as a haven of refuge, but as a port of call, and repeatedly pressed the government for permission to exploit it. Despite fierce opposition from the established ports of Truro, Penryn and Helston, new quays were constructed, and a custom house build here to replace the one at Penryn. In 1660 Smithwick became Falmouth, and the place received its charter a year later.

The behaviour of the Killigrews was sometimes outrageous. John Killigrew, who became the first governor of Pendennis Castle in 1546, engaged in piracy; a practice which led him to serving time in London's Fleet Prison with his son John. This son, who was also to become a governor at Pendennis, was knighted by Elizabeth I. By a strange quirk of fate he was appointed chairman of the Commissioners for Piracy in Cornwall; a situation which had its advantages for his wife, Lady Mary, who, accused of plundering a Spanish ship and murdering its crew, walked free, while others were hanged. The third John Killigrew was another ne'er do well governor of Pendennis who ended his days in prison, but the fourth was more reliable, building Cornwall's first lighthouse, at the Lizard (see no. 79).

The estate was inherited in 1633 by his brother, Sir Peter, a staunch Royalist instrumental in obtaining Falmouth's charter in 1661. It was his son, also Sir Peter, who built Town Quay, now known as Custom House Quay. It seemed the end of the line after the death in infancy of his eldest son, Peter, and the loss of his second son, George in a brawl. Then Martin Lister, who married Anne Killigrew, adopted the family name in the hope of producing a son and heir – but this was not to be. So instead he decided to erect this obelisk, asking that it bear no inscription, but hoping it would remain 'a beauty to the Harbour without limitation of time.' Inside, about half way up, is a sealed bottle containing historic information, as directed by a subsequent Manor Bailiff. Yet higher is another bottle, surreptitiously placed there by the workmen.

Places of Interest in the Neighbourhood
41. A 17th Century Fire Engine
42. Saluting the Men of Falmouth's Post Office Packet Service
44. The King's Pipe
45. Four Bunks for Five

44 The King's Pipe

Position: The King's Pipe, on the steep approach to Custom House Quay from Arwenack Street, Falmouth
Ordnance Map: Truro, Falmouth & surrounding area: Landranger 204 1:50 000
Map Ref: SW/811/324

Note: The strange looking four tiered chimney stack adjacent to the handsome Customs House and known by the intriguing name of The King's Pipe, was built for the burning of contraband tobacco. It probably dates from around 1814, when the Custom House, with its noble Doric pillars facing Arwenack Street was constructed. The grand facade, with its Coat of Arms, contrasts with the more work-a-day seaward side, which, built on the slope, has two storeys.

A sharp eyed Falmouth Preventive Officer named Bright, who boarded the suspect schooner *Marie Victoire* in the harbour in May 1839, insisted on remaining aboard as she proceeded up river to Malpas, where her markedly cool and nonchalent crew set about unloading her cargo of coal, leaving him to bore away with his gimlet. Finally a telltale jet of brandy shot out of a concealed cask, and further investigations revealed a false bottom, stacked with spirits. When Bright looked around, the entire ship's company had vanished.

Places of Interest in the Neighbourhood
41. A 17th Century Fire Engine
42. Saluting the Men of Falmouth's Post Office Packet Service
43. 'A Beauty to the Harbour without Limitation of Time . . .'
45. Four Bunks for Five

St Denys, *Custom House Quay, Truro*

45 Four Bunks for Five

Position: Steam Tug *St Denys*, alongside Custom House Quay
Ordnance Map: Truro, Falmouth & surrounding area: Sheet 204 1:50 000
Map Ref: SW/811/324

Note: The steam tug *St Denys*, anchored alongside Custom House
Quay, spent all her working life in the port of Falmouth and was
acquired by the Maritime Museum in 1981 when due for the scrapyard.
She is unique in possessing the only remaining Caprotti valve marine
steam engine in existence. Although superstition would deem it
unlucky to change the name of a ship or a house, this vessel, built at
Dalmuir in 1929 for the Falmouth Towage Company and originally
known as the *Northgate Scott*, acquired her saintly name in 1959,when
all the port's tugs were similarly honouring the Cornish saints.

The captain and chief officer's cabins off the day saloon were
considerably more comfortable than the crew's quarters, where, with
one man always on duty, it was a case of the four bunks being kept
warm by five men.

The captain used a megaphone to instruct those on deck, and a
telegraph and voice pipe to contact the engine room. The ship's wheel,
apparently facing the stern, was positioned to offer maximum visibility
and freedom of movement when towing. The rudder system, operated
by rods and chains, was backed up by a tiller at the stern for emergency
use. But as far as local folk are concerned, the tug's most memorable
feat was to propel a spectacular jet of water to the Recreation Ground,
200 feet high and half a mile distant, when moored at Prince of Wales
Pier during the last war.

Places of Interest in the Neighbourhood
41. A 17th Century Fire Engine
42. Saluting the Men of Falmouth's Post Office Packet Service
43. 'A Beauty to the Harbour without Limitation of Time . . .'
44. The King's Pipe

46 'The Cornish Wonder'

Position: Harmony Cottage, to the east of St Agnes, between Mithian
& Trevellas
Ordnance Map: Truro, Falmouth & surrounding area: Sheet 204 1:50 000
Map Ref: SW/745/514

Note: Harmony Cottage was the birthplace in 1761 of John Opie, the
son of a carpenter and a self-taught artist with a particular affinity
towards portraiture. At the age of 15 he met John Wolcot, who
sponsored him, tutored him and took him to London, where he moved
in high society and became the most fashionable portrait painter of the
decade, nicknamed 'The Cornish Wonder.' He was elected to the
Royal Academy in 1787, and was buried in St Paul's Cathedral.
Altogether he produced about 750 paintings, some of which can be
seen in the National Portrait Gallery. Interestingly, the only portrait of
John Knill was produced by John Opie, in 1779, before both left the
county for London.

Places of Interest in the Neighbourhood
47. 'The Pepper Pot'
48. Crowning Glory
49. When 'The horses stayed still, the wheels went around . . .'
50. A Monument to 'Knackt Bals'

47 'The Pepper Pot'

Position: Above the harbour at Portreath
Ordnance Map: Land's End & The Lizard: Sheet 203 1:50 000
Map Ref: SW/655/456

Note: Portreath, with its docks and railway serving the tin and copper mining areas of St Day, was transformed from a little fishing village by Francis Basset of the mine owning Bassets of Tehidy.

During the last century it grew into a busy port, exporting copper ore to Swansea for smelting, and importing coal and timber for the mines. But as the harbour entrance proved to be rather narrow and dangerous, a daymark was erected to assist vessels entering the little port. This pleasing white, conical tower 123 feet above high water, and 25 feet high, became affectionately known as 'The Pepper Pot'. After dark a tidal light shone red when the port was accessible and green when it was not.

Places of Interest in the Neighbourhood
46. 'The Cornish Wonder'
48. Crowning Glory
49. When 'The horses stayed still, the wheels went around . . .'
50. A Monument to 'Knackt Bals'

48 Crowning Glory

Position: Carn Brea, to the south west of Redruth
Ordnance Map: Land's End & The Lizard: Sheet 203 :1:50 000
Map Ref: SW/686/408
Access: Footpaths up the northern side, from secondary roads between
Redruth and Camborne. Accessible by car from the village of Carnkie,
to the south.

Note: The curiously shaped Carn Brea, seen in dramatic profile above
Redruth against the setting sun, is said to house the giant Bolster, who
can nonchalently place one foot on Carn Brea and the other on St
Agnes Beacon. Somehow it seems fitting that the inventive genius
Richard Trevithick was born within the shadow of Carn Brea in 1771.

The summit is topped by an extraordinary monument of 1836, to the
memory of Francis, Lord St Dunstanville, one of the wealthy Bassets of
Tehidy, who had extensive mining interests throughout the area (see
No. 47). Just along the ridge, a sham castle built into a rocky outcrop,
now a restaurant, may have originally been an Elizabethan hunting
lodge.

The summit of Carn Brea commands magnificent views, and it has
long been one of the Beacons on which bonfires were lit in times of
strife or celebration. Along the foot of this massive granite beacon is a
dense network of 'knackt bals' (defunct mines), once described as
Cornwall's 'Black Country,' amongst them the famous Dolcoath mine,
where men worked half a mile below the surface to extract tin and
copper ore.

Places of Interest in the Neighbourhood
46. 'The Cornish Wonder'
47. 'The Pepper Pot'
49. When 'The horses stayed still, the wheels went around . . .'
50. A Monument to 'Knackt Bals'

The Castle, Carn Brae

49 When 'The horses stayed still, the wheels went around . . .'

Position: Opposite the Free Library in Camborne
Ordnance Map: Land's End & The Lizard: Sheet 203 1:50 000
Map Ref: SW/651/395

Note: The sculptor L. E. Merrifield's bronze statue outside Camborne's public library depicting that restless, inventive Cornish genius Richard Trevithick in swallow tailed coat and breeches, looking up Beacon Hill, clasping a steam locomotive in one hand and a pair of dividers in the other, symbolises the exciting happenings here on the Christmas Eve of 1801 which became immortalised in the Cornish song:

> Going up Camborne Hill, coming down,
> Going up Camborne Hill, coming down;
> The horses stayed still, the wheels went around,
> Going up Camborne Hill, coming down!

After making experimental models of high pressure steam engines it was here that a trial run of Britain's first full sized road locomotive took place. Horse drawn vehicles came to a standstill at the spectacle which gave rise to the song, as the 'Puffing devil' transported ten or so volunteers at more than walking pace. There is also a plaque to mark the site where the first locomotive was assembled and set out for the trial run. A monument was erected to Richard Trevithick (1771-1833) at his birthplace in Illogan, and there is a fine marble bust of him sculpted by Nevil Northey Burnard in the Royal Institution of Cornwall (Truro Museum). Camborne Museum has a Trevithick display and there is a Trevithick Society. Camborne celebrates Trevithick Day in April with a procession of dancers and steam engines through the streets.

Richard Trevithick was born at a time when alluvial mining was being exhausted in Cornwall and mine shafts were deepening, making it harder to remove the water. He applied his skills to the improvement of mine pumps and developed a wide variety of devices ranging from powering mills to paddle wheel barges. His work took him to London and later to the Peruvian Silver Mines and the bells of Camborne church pealed out a welcome on his return. He died while working at Dartford in Kent, where he was buried.

Places of Interest in the Neighbourhood
46. 'The Cornish Wonder'
47. 'The Pepper Pot'
48. Crowning Glory
50. A Monument to 'Knackt Bals'

50 A Monument to 'Knackt Bals'

Position: Cornish Engine House at East Pool, & other impressive relics of the tin mining industry on either side of the A3047, 2 miles west of Redruth [NT]
Ordnance Map: Land's End & The Lizard: Sheet 203 1:50 000
Map Ref: SW/672/415

Note: The attractively designed engine house at East Pool was typical of hundreds built to house the great beam engines used for pumping water and for winding men and ore. One beam engine here has a cylinder 7½ feet in diameter, used for pumping water from a depth of over 2,000 feet. It recalls the work of Richard Trevithick (see No. 49), and the high pressure steam engines he patented. Many such engine houses dot the landscape, and now ruined are sometimes referred to as 'Cornish Castles'.

The 90 inch cylinder pumping engine at Taylor's Shaft, East Pool and Agar Mine, Pool, built by the famous engineering firm, Harvey's of Hayle in 1892, has been restored by the Cornish Engines Preservation Society and is now in the care of the National Trust. Initially metal ores were extracted by streaming and alluvial methods, working on the surface, but as these deposits ran out viable means had to be found to exploit the lodes at ever deepening levels. One of the biggest problems was to remove the quantities of water which invariably flooded the workings, and this was done by muscle power, windmills and water wheels. But the breakthrough came with the invention of steam pumps, which evolved from Thomas Savary's simple 'Miner's Friend', and fellow Devonian Thomas Newcomen's early steam engine. The colloquial expression 'knackt bals', always depressing news for Cornishmen, meant simply mining in recession.

Places of Interest in the Neighbourhood
46. 'The Cornish Wonder'
47. 'The Pepper Pot'
48. Crowning Glory
49. When 'The horses stayed still, the wheels went around . . .'

51 An Island Lighthouse which lent its Name to a Novel

Position: Lighthouse on Godrevy Island off Godrevy Point, on the eastern side of St Ives Bay
Ordnance Map: Land's End & The Lizard: Sheet 203 1:50 000
Map Ref: SW/577/436
Access: From the A3301, follow the signposts to Godrevy Towans to the north of Gwithian

Note: Over many centuries the partly submerged reef of rocks, somewhat innocuously known as The Stones, has become a notorious graveyard for a host of ships.

One of the earliest disasters to be documented, and also one of the most remarkable co-incidental happenings took place on 30th January 1639. For on this fateful day Charles I was executed, and by a strange chance the Topsham vessel *Garland*, carrying his wardrobe and possessions as well as that of his fugitive queen, was dashed to pieces on The Stones in a storm. Of the sixty or so people aboard, all were lost apart from a man, a boy and a dog who swam to the island and survived on seaweed and rainwater before being rescued. Some say that the queen's jewels were discovered by a humble cottager on Gwithian beach a few days later.

The Stones have given rise to a seemingly endless catalogue of disasters. But it was the dramatic wrecking of the iron-screw passenger steamer *Nile* in 1854, in which all aboard lost their lives, that led to a navigational light being set up.

The *Nile*, which traded between Liverpool, Cornish ports and London, had been delayed by bad weather. Whilst off the north Cornish coast she was driven eastwards in poor visibility and fading light, striking the Deeper Stones at speed, breaking up and littering the shore with bodies and the debris of ship and cargo. Trinity House responded promptly to the disaster, announcing its intention to have a lighthouse erected here. Although the principle had always been to site warning lights as near the hazard as possible, the cost of building on The Stones was considered prohibitive, so the alternatives of St Ives Headland or Godrevy Island were considered. Two further ships were lost before the decision was finally made.

The lighthouse, which first cast its light across these treacherous waters on 1st March, 1859, just before completion, was designed by Trinity House engineer James Walker, and was built by Thomas Eva and Thomas Williams of Helston. Since that time the number of

82

shipwrecks has lessened. The engaging sight of Godrevy Lighthouse on its own little island has delighted generations of families on holiday in the area, and so inspired the writer Virginia Woolf that she incorporated it in the title of her 'stream of consciousness' novel *To The Lighthouse*.

Places of Interest in the Neighbourhood
52. 'Knill's Steeple'
53. The Eddystone Connection with St Ives
54. The Rag and Bone Artist

52 'Knill's Steeple'

Position: The Knill Monument, on Worvas Hill, St Ives
Ordnance Map: Land's End & The Lizard: Sheet 203 1:50 000
Map Ref: SW/516/387

Note: The granite memorial on the top of Worvas Hill, which forms a prominent landmark for shipping, colloquially known as 'Knill's Steeple', is a much loved monument to eccentricity, erected by John Knill, an 18th century Customs Officer, unofficial smuggler and Mayor, but intended as his mausoleum. As so often happened in these cases of post mortal ambition, he died elsewhere and the sarcophagus remained empty. On one face of the pyramid there appears *Resurgam*, with the Knill Coat of Arms and the punning motto *Nil Desperandum*; on the other sides 'I know that my Redeemer Liveth' and 'Johannes Knill 1782.' But this painful pun was not his only piece of posterial fun. He made provision in his will for a peculiar quinquennial (5 yearly) celebration, whereby on St James' Day, 25th June, ten little girls aged ten and dressed in white, accompanied by two widows, a clergyman, fiddler, customs officer and Mayor of St Ives, were to sing the Old Hundredth Psalm, then dance and sing for fifteen minutes to the fiddler (to the tune of 'Boy and Girls Come Out To Play')

'Shun the bustle of the bay,
Hasten virgins, come away:
Hasten to the mountain's brow,
Leave, oh leave St Ives below.
Haste to breathe a purer air,
Virgins fair, and pure as fair;
Fly St Ives and all her treasures,
Fly her soft voluptuous pleasures,
Fly her sons and all the wiles
Lurking in their wanton smiles
Fly her splendid midnight halls
Fly the revels of her balls;
Fly; oh fly, the chosen seat
Where vanity and fashion meet.
Thither hasten, form the ring,
Round the tomb in chorus sing.
And on the loft mountain's brow aptly dight,
Just as we should be, all in white,
Leave all our cowels and our cares below.

Places of Interest in the Neighbourhood

51. An Island Lighthouse which lent its Name to a Novel
53. The Eddystone Connection with St Ives
54. The Rag and Bone Artist

53 The Eddystone Connection with St Ives

Position: Smeaton Pier, St Ives
Ordnance Map: Land's End & The Lizard: Sheet 203 1:50 000
Map Ref: SW/521/406

Note: It was the colourful one time Mayor of St Ives, John Knill (see No. 52), who sought the advice of John Smeaton, builder of the Eddystone Lighthouse, on the building of a pier to protect the port's fishing vessels in 1770. The attractive lighthouse built on the end of Smeaton's Pier in 1831 replaced the former lantern on a pole, which had served as a quayhead light.

In 1857 'a St Ives Man Born and Bred' issued a poster proclaiming that: 'The commissioners of the St Ives New Pier Act will please Take Notice that it is the intention of the Inhabitants of this Town to have a NEW PIER . . .' And it issued a rallying cry for townsfolk to get together and raise money themselves, pointing out 'NO PIER, NO PROSPERITY.' Unfortunately this New or Wood Pier, running out from the Castle Rocks on the seaward side of Smeaton's Pier, became a victim of the pounding Atlantic storms, so all that remains is a small stump, whilst its lamp can be seeen in the museum. The West Pier, originally built for the exporting of roadstone, was completed in 1894.

The old fishermen's Chapel of St Nicholas at the point of Pendinas (The Island) has had a chequered history, having been used as a look out for Customs men, a refuge for pilots and a wartime store, before being demolished by the War Office and re-erected by Sir Edward Hain in 1911. John Leland, the King's topographer recorded this chapel on the point, together with 'a pharos for lighte for shippes sailing by night in these quarters.'

Places of Interest in the Neighbourhood
51. An Island Lighthouse which lent its Name to a Novel
52. 'Knill's Steeple'
54. The Rag and Bone Artist

54 The Rag and Bone Artist

Position: Plaque to Alfred Wallis on the wall of Harry's Court, Back
Road West, St Ives
Ordnance Map: Land's End & The Lizard: Sheet 203 1:50 000
Map Ref: SW/515/405

Note: The simple plaque on the wall of 3 Back Road West recalls
Alfred Wallis, the unassuming rag and bone man, who, at a time when
St Ives was attracting sophisticated artists, painted in his own
apparently simple, but colourful and compelling style for the sheer joy
of it, was ridiculed, then proclaimed an 'untutored genius'.

This shy, withdrawn man was born poor in 1855 and lost his mother
when still young. He claimed to have been a cabin boy aged nine, on
the Newfoundland run from Penzance and Newlyn, before joining the
Mousehole and Newlyn fishing fleets, and much of his work depicted
fishing boats. Arriving in St Ives in 1890 as a rag and bone man,
married to a widow twenty one years his senior who reputedly already
had seventeen children, he established himself first at Bethesda Hill,
then on the waterfront, from where he walked the streets with his cart,

crying out for scrap metal. After moving to Back Road West and losing his wife, he turned more and more to painting 'for company'. Unlike the trained painters, who conspicuously set up their easels out of doors when the sun shone, he worked indoors painting 'out of my own memery' on a flat table in the light of the open doorway on scraps of paper and cardboard of irregular shape, incorporating the shape as part of the art, instead of squaring it off. He used marine paint, which he understood, and familiar brushes which he felt at home with, rather than the recognised equipment. It was thus that he first came to the attention of Christopher Wood, Sven Berlin and others, who recognised his genius and tried to help him reach a larger audience. But Wallis never demanded fair prices for his work, despite his perpetual dread of ending up in the workhouse and being buried in a pauper's grave. This fear ended with the awful reality of being taken into Madron Workhouse, where he died in 1942. His grave in Porthmeor Cemetery, St Ives, bears the simple inscription 'Alfred Wallis, Artist and Mariner.' But a floral tribute of the time from Nuam Gabo summed it up rather more poignantly with the dedication: 'In homage to the artist on whom Nature has bestowed the rarest of gifts, not to know that he is one.'

Places of Interest in the Neighbourhood
51. An Island Lighthouse which lent its Name to a Novel
52. 'Knill's Steeple'
53. The Eddystone Connection with St Ives

Alfred Wallis

55 The Old Engine Houses

Position: Along the coastline at Botallack, to the north of St Just in Penwith
Ordnance Map: Land's End & The Lizard: Sheet 203 1:50 000
Map Ref: SW/362/336

Note: The picturesque ruins of Botallack's old engine houses and mine workings are perched dramatically on the rocks, with the Atlantic far below. For centuries miners have worked these concentrated mineralised lodes, which in Wheal Cock and the Crowns extended a considerable distance out under the sea. After visits by royalty around the middle of the last century, it became the fashionable thing for writers, artists and notable people to come here and witness the marvels for themselves. For at that time the almost legendary maze of platforms, ladders and machinery descending the cliffs was a source of wonder. 'Who?' asked 'Esquiros' in 1824, 'would not admire, at Botallack mine, the grandeur of industry with the grandeur of nature?'

Another writer, J. A. Paris, was more sympathetic to the miners themselves: 'The workings of this mine extend at least seventy fathoms in length under the bed of the sea; and in these caverns of darkness are many human beings, for a small pittance, and even that of a precarious amount, constantly digging for ore, regardless of the horrors which surround them, and the roar of the Atlantic ocean, whose boisterious waves are incessantly rolling over their heads. We should feel pity for the wretch who, as an atonement for his crimes, should be compelled to undergo the tasks which the Cornish miner voluntarily undertakes and as cheerfully performs.'

Places of Interest in the Neighbourhood
57. The Capstan House and the Caunse

56 The Merry Maidens of Boleigh, and their Pipers

Position: Close to the B3315 Newlyn to Land's End road, just beyond the farm at Trewoofe. Both visible from the road, the Merry Maidens are on the left, and The Pipers on the right. Look for the signposted footpath to the Merry Maidens.
Ordnance Map: Land's End & The Lizard: Sheet 203 1:50 000
Map Ref: SW/435/245

Note: The impressive 80 feet circle of 19 stones, each standing about 4 feet high, were obviously carefully set in place, perhaps during the Bronze Age. It is likely that they played a role in pagan religious rites, the significance of which has been lost down the centuries. But folklore would have us believe that these stones remain as a perpetual and salutary reminder of Divine displeasure. The story goes that nineteen comely maidens, full of the joy and high spiritedness of youth, forgot about attending Sunday vespers, and strayed into these fields, laughing and chattering, and that they started dancing to the lively music of the pipers; the Pipers in question being the two, quarter mile distant, tall, standing stones. Suddenly there was a mighty flash, which transfixed for ever the Merry Maidens and their Pipers for the sin of dancing on the Sabbath Day.

Places of Interest in the Neighbourhood
58. The Theatre on the Cliffs
59. Trounced on his own Doorstep
60. The Ring and Thimble Monument
61. The Last Speaker of the Cornish Language?

57 The Capstan House and the Caunse

Position: The slipway at Sennen Cove
Ordnance Map: Land's End & The Lizard: Sheet 203 1:50 000
Map Ref: SW/351/264

Note: The most unusual building at Sennen Cove has to be the round
capstan house, with its conical roof originally built to cover the huge
capstan (still *in situ*), used for hauling the fishing boats up the slipway.
It was later used as a fishing store, and is now a protected building.

Life was never easy at Sennen, and sea conditions hampered the
launching and beaching of boats until the present harbour was built.
This involved cutting back the cliff and clearing boulders to create a
slipway of flat granite rocks, 120 feet wide, which became known as the
Caunse.

The need to create effective shelter was brought home by the
wrecking of the barque *Khyber* at Tol Pedn in March 1905 in furious
seas, when the Sennen lifeboat could not be launched. Two plaques on
the breakwater tell of those involved with the subsequent money
raising efforts. Lord Falmouth, who was responsible for the capstan
and rope, enjoyed an entitlement to the second best fish and the worst
of every catch.

Places of Interest in the Neighbourhood
55. The old Engine Houses
58. The Theatre on the Cliffs

58 The Theatre on the Cliffs

Position: The Minack Open Air Theatre, Porthcurno
Ordnance Map: Land's End & The Lizard: Sheet 203 1:50 000
Map Ref: SW/387/221
Access: From the B3315 Newlyn to Lands End road, turn left to
Porthcurno, then follow the road to the clifftop

Note: To the whimsical imagination, the open air theatre which so
pleasingly graces the cliffs at Porthcurno might have been created
thousands of years ago by some passing Greek. For below a semi-
circular auditorium there is a stage of classical style with pillars and
archways against a backdrop of sea and sky.

Once a grassy gully, it was a Miss Rowena Cade who saw its potential
as an open air theatre in the 1930s and who loving worked to turn it into
a reality. In 1932 The *Tempest* was staged with plays every two years
until the outbreak of war, when it was wreathed in barbed wire and
crowned by an anti-aircraft gun emplacement, later to become a box
office. Although it seemed unlikely that it could ever function as a
theatre again, the film *Love Story*, with Margaret Lockwood and
Stewart Granger was made here in 1944. After the war Dame Sybil
Thorndike was founder President and Dame Flora Robson Vice
President. It soon attracted many distinguished actors and actresses,
and remains a favourite venue today, with an enthusiastic following.

Places of Interest in the Neighbourhood
59. Trounced on his own Doorstep
60. The Ring and Thimble Monument
61. The Last Speaker of the Cornish Language?
62. A now Historic Piece of Artistic Licence

59 Trounced on his Own Doorstep

Position: Keigwin House in Keigwin Street, Mousehole
Ordnance Map: Land's End & The Lizard: Sheet 203 1:50 000
Map Ref: SW/469/264

Note:

> 'Strangers will land on the rocks of Merlin,
> Who will burn Paul church, Penzance and Newlyn'

ran the prophetic old rhyme. But when the inhabitants of Mousehole awoke one July morning in 1595 to find four Spanish men o'war anchored just off those rocks, and several boatloads of armed men coming ashore, they were totally unprepared. The Spaniards sacked and plundered the village, before setting Paul church ablaze and marching on Newlyn and Penzance.

This pleasing, 16th century manor house with a fine, overhanging porch and granite pillars is supposedly the only building in Mousehole to have withstood the attack. Furthermore, the story goes that the proud and patriotic Jenkin Keigwin, who stoutly defended the place and brought down some Spaniards with a blast from his musket, was himself blown to eternity by a Spanish cannon ball on his own doorstep. According to popular folklore, ghosts of the influential Keigwin family occasionally appear on the stairs in stately attire and fully armed.

Places of Interest in the Neighbourhood
58. The Theatre on the Cliffs
60. The Ring and Thimble Monument
61. The Last Speaker of the Cornish Language?
62. A now Historic Piece of Artistic Licence
63. The Voyage of the *Mystery*

60 The Ring and Thimble Monument

Position: Ring and Thimble Monument at the top of Chywoone Hill, Newlyn
Ordnance Map: Land's End & The Lizard: Sheet 203 1:50 000
Map Ref: SW/460/278

Note: A certain amount of mystery surrounds this strange little monument resembling a ring and thimble. It was built by John Price of Kerris, four times Mayor of Penzance in the latter part of the 18th century, whose family had made a fortune out of the Jamaican sugar plantations. Some think that the monument, heavy in symbolism, was erected as a memorial to a young daughter of the Price family, who died in a riding accident, and who therefore was never to experience nuptial bliss. Stranger still was the account of the woodcutter who came upon a ring and thimble embedded in the very heart of a tree trunk. Not only that, but it bore the motto *In hac spe vivo*, which was interpreted by some as the prophetic 'in hacking wood I found a ring,' and by others as 'in this lives hope'. Next to the stone with its carved circle, John Price placed a conical stone, resembling a sugar loaf in homage to the family fortune, but interpreted around these parts as a thimble, completing the fertility symbol.

This little known, intriguing little monument, formerly overgrown and sinking into oblivion, owes its re-emerged glory to the County Highways Department, who came across it during road widening work in 1989. *In hac spe vivo*, as they say.

Places of Interest in the Neighbourhood

61 The Last Speaker of the Cornish Language?

Position: Dolly Pentreath's memorial stone, in the outer wall of Paul churchyard
Ordnance Map: Land's End & The Lizard: Sheet 203 1:50 000
Map Ref: SW/465/272
Access: From the B3315 from Newlyn to Land's End, look for the signpost on the left to Paul, just outside Newlyn.

Note: The unusual monument set in the outer wall of Paul churchyard pays homage to Dolly Pentreath, a native of Mousehole who died in 1777, and whom, according to popular folklore was the last speaker of the Cornish language; a claim which has been widely contested. For William Bodenor in the same churchyard has been cited as a later speaker of Cornish, while John Davey of Boswednack, near Zennor (1812-92), might well claim this distinction. Some say that Dolly stole the limelight by jabbering some words of ancient Cornish to impress folk, if the price was right, and cursing them for nothing if it were not.

The story of how the stone came to be here is almost as bizarre. Being near the fashionable watering place of Penzance, well-heeled

visitors, including royalty found their way to the quaint local villages, some staying at the inn here. One such was Prince Louis Lucien Bonaparte, an antiquarian linguist, who, intrigued by the folklore surrounding Dolly, decided with the Rev John Garrett, vicar of St Paul, to erect this stone in her honour, with a lengthy and partly irrelevant inscription.

Clearly local folk felt that the Prince had been carried away. With tongue in cheek, *The West Briton* in March 1888 reported: 'Poor old Dolly Pentreath's grave has been found in Paul's churchyard, and the big memorial stone erected by Prince Lucien Bonaparte in the wrong place has been transferred to where the bones rest of the last talker of old Cornish. Dolly's head was of a peculiar shape, judging by the skull which has now come to the surface, and it shows how hard the old soul worked at the Cornish language, for only three teeth were found.'

Places of Interest in the Neighbourhood

62 A now Historic Piece of Artistic Licence

Position: Le Rue Des Beaux Arts, Newlyn
Ordnance Map: Land's End & The Lizard: Sheet 203 1:50 000
Map Ref: SW/464/285
Access: Half way up Trewarveneth Street, to the left

Note: Le Rue des Beaux Arts, lying parallel to one of the narrow streets straggling up the hillside above the old port of Newlyn, recalls the colony of artists who gravitated here in the latter part of the last century, attracted by the particularly clear quality of the light, the colourful boats, and picturesque work-a-day charm of its fisherfolk. Known collectively as the Newlyn School, they took over some of the fishermen's cottages among the quaint courts and alleyways, which have a kind of Continental charm. The artists built up quite a good rapport with the fisherfolk, some of whom modelled for them as they painted out of doors, or were employed in copper repoussé work, combining the functional with the beautiful. No one knows who actually decided to rename this lane, by the simple expedient of lettering out the signboard and fixing it to the side of the cottage, but A.G. Folliot Stokes writing in 1909 warms rather engagingly to the theme, suggesting that it 'originated in the brain of an artist who, many years ago, fresh from Paris and the haunting fascination of the Quartier Latin, conceived the idea of thus naming one of these little alleys. Being a man of action as well as of artistic temperament – two qualities that by no means always go together – he promptly painted upon a board in large letters the name of this famous thoroughfare and fixed it to a corner of an old house. Inexplicably, attempts were made to demolish some of these much loved cottages just before the last war in the name of slum clearance. A deputation of fishermen sailed around the coast and up the Thames to the Houses of Parliament in the long liner *Rosebud*, to present a petition. But it was really the outbreak of the Second World War that brought the clearance to a halt.

Today both houses and paintings fetch very high prices.

Places of Interest in the Neighbourhood
58. The Theatre on the Cliffs
59. Trounced on his own Doorstep
60. The Ring and Thimble Monument
61. The Last Speaker of the Cornish Language?

63 The Voyage of the *Mystery*

Position: Mystery plaque outside the Mission To Deep Sea Fishermen
in Newlyn
Ordnance Map: Land's End & The Lizard: Sheet 203 1:50 000
Map Ref: SW/463/290

Note: The plaque outside Newlyn's Mission To Deep Sea Fishermen
depicting a small lugger recalls a colourful local adventure at the time
of the Gold Rush, involving a feat of seamanship unparalleled at the
time.

Following Charles Kelynack's departure to Australia to try his luck
in the goldfields, the crew of the family owned fishing lugger *Mystery*
who were keen to join him had plans to sell the boat in order to raise the
passage money. But the combined circumstances of Richard Nicholls,
captain of a Welsh trader coming home on leave, meeting up with his
mates and having more than a few pints of ale in a Penzance inn,
somehow led to the idea of them sailing to Australia in their own boat,
with Richard acting as skipper. Few such schemes survive the cold light
of morning, but neither Richard Nicholls, Job Kelynack, William
Badcock, Richard Badcock, Charles Boase, Philip Matthews nor
Lewis Lewis was going to be the first to back down, And so it went
ahead.

They made various adaptations to their 36 feet lugger, such as
sheathing her bottom with zinc plates and decking her fore and aft, and
took on a supply of fresh water and provisions including salted meat
and hard tack. On 18th November 1854 they set sail, with only a
compass, sextant and barometer for navigation, cheered off by
enthusiastic crowds on the shore and in escorting boats.

During the epic voyage they experienced everything the sea had to
offer; ranging from being caught in the doldrums to anchoring to a
launched raft as a safety measure against the fury of storms. It was 4
months before their families and friends heard of their safe arrival in
Cape Town, where they became the centre of much interesf.

They were warmly welcomed on their arrival in Melbourne on 14th
March 1855, when a St Just man left the goldfields for a sight of them,
and Captain Price RN, son of Sir Rose Price of Trengwainton near
Newlyn, offered hospitality. So the splendid adventure, hatched in a
heady mood in a Penzance inn was safely completed after 116 days at
sea. And what about striking it rich in the goldfields? Well, they
seemed to have forgotten about that in all the excitement, possibly
subscribing to the theory that it is better to travel hopefully.

Most of them eventually returned to Newlyn. It is perhaps ironical that Captain Nicholls was to lose his life as a result of being knocked down by a London cab.

The log of the *Mystery* is now housed at the Royal Institution of Cornwall in Truro (Truro Museum), where there is also a scale model of the ship, made by Joseph Carter, the husband of William Badcock's daughter, Harriet.

A plaque of 1987, to the right, recalls the *Rosebud* exploit (see No. 62).

Places of Interest in the Neighbourhood
58. The Theatre on the Cliffs
59. Trounced on his own Doorstep
60. The Ring and Thimble Monument
61. The Last Speaker of the Cornish Language?
62. A now Historic Piece of Artistic Licence

64 A Punning Device

Position: The old Town Seal on the wall of the Market House at the top
of Market Jew Street, Penzance
Ordnance Map: Land's End & The Lizard: Sheet 203 1:50 000
Map Ref: SW/473/304

Note: The relief picture of a head on a platter, to be found on the side of
the Market House, is a depiction of the town's Borough Seal of 1614.

The original name *'Pens Sans'* meant Holy Headland, and referred
to a headland, long eroded away by the sea, on which stood a tiny
chapel dedicated to St Anthony. When it came to choosing a Seal, at
the time of their Charter, granted by James I in 1614, the townsfolk
opted for this punning device depicting St John the Baptist's holy head
on a charger. Furthermore, Madron, once the site of their mother
church, was an early possession of the Knights of St John, whose badge
depicted St John's head on a charger.

Penzance recovered from a devastating attack from the Spaniards in
1595 to achieve Borough status within twenty years. It went on to
exploit its trading potential by land and sea, ousting Marazion as the
area's principal marketing centre. The first Market House was erected
on this site at the top of Market Jew Street, and was replaced in 1836.
In 1663 it acquired the additional status of a coinage town, where tin
was brought for testing and assessed for taxes.

In 1974, after 360 years of corporate existence, with expansion in
1934, Penzance lost its Borough status, becoming part of the County
District of Penwith. The new Town Badge retains this punning theme.

Places of Interest in the Neighbourhood

65 Penzance's Library in a Garden

Position: Private Lending Library, in Morrab House, situated in the
Morrab Gardens, off Morrab Road, Penzance
Ordnance Map: Land's End & The Lizard: Sheet 203 1:50 000
Map Ref: SW/473/298

Note: The Penzance Library, a unique and prestigious Cornish
institution, with a notable collection of early and rare books, first
editions of famous works, manuscripts, paintings, drawings,
engravings, photographs, archive newspapers and a comprehensive
Cornish section, is one of the few remaining private lending libraries
left in Britain. Its particularly pleasing setting led that literary son of
Cornwall, Sir Arthur Quiller Couch to write: 'There are hundreds of
bigger libraries, but few have a pleasanter tradition, and not one is so
beautifully placed. Can a bookish person imagine anything more
delightful than a library put together by the taste and care of
generations of scholars and students and set in a garden by the sea?'

The library had several homes before it settled into its present
situation a century ago. It started as a small collection of books kept in
Cumming's Hotel in the Market Place in 1818. Ten years later the
collection was moved to the first floor of the Commercial Buildings in
Parade Street, where they remained for forty years, before moving to
the Public Buildings in Alverton Street in 1867.

One early committee member listening to the president and
treasurer mumbling their way through a meeting at the other end of the
table, suggested, 'Gentlemen, I have to propose that the committee
votes the money to purchase three dozen marbles, half stoners and half
clayers, in order that the members at this end of the table may have
something with which to occupy themselves from going to sleep.' The
Library moved into Morrab House, which had been built by Samuel
Pidwell, a year after the Corporation acquired the property and set
about creating the beautiful sub tropical gardens in 1888. The Library,
originally known as The Penzance Library at the time of its formation
in 1818, but later called The Penzance Public Library, reverted to its
original name after moving here at the end of 1889.

Places of Interest in the Neighbourhood
66. Cornwall's most Bizarre Building in a Street of Curiosities
67. At the End of its Tether
68. 'The Hoar Rock in the Wood'
69. A Causeway financed by Sinners

66 Cornwall's most Bizarre Building in a Street of Curiosities

Position: The Egyptian House near the top of Chapel Street, Penzance
Ordnance Map: Land's End & The Lizard: Sheet 203 1:50 000
Map Ref: SW/474/302

Note: The Egyptian House in this street of notable buildings, must be the most bizarre to be found in Cornwall. It was built in 1835/6 by John Foulston, as a follow up to his similarly inspired design of the Classical School in Devonport in 1832 to house the mineral collection of John Lavin, who occupied the house for some years. The extremely flamboyant façade has lotus columns, angled contours and extravagant ornamentation, with sphinx like ladies, and a somewhat incongruous lion and unicorn lending a touch of Empire to the Orient.

After years of neglect, this building was restored in 1973 by the Landmark Trust. The Royal Arms are of the period of George III and William IV. The ground floor is used as a National Trust shop.

Other buildings of particular interest in this street of curiosities, include the Union Hotel, where news of Nelson's victory at Trafalgar was first announced, and above whose stables is a lovely little Georgian theatre, the *Admiral Benbow Inn*, which has a seaward looking pirate lurking on its roof and nautical decor inside, and the *Turk's Head Inn*, the oldest in Penzance, which has colourful seafaring and piratical associations.

Places of Interest in the Neighbourhood

105

67 At the End of its Tether

Position: Celtic Cross, outside Penlee Museum, Penzance
Ordnance Map: Land's End & The Lizard: Sheet 203 1:50 000
Map Ref: SW/472/300

Note: The handsome Celtic cross just outside Penlee Museum bears the proud inscription *Hic Procumbant Corpora Piorum et Regis Ricati Crux* (the cross of King Ricatus). This cross has for centuries been an essential part of the Penzance scene, having variously occupied sites at the bottom of Causewayhead, outside the Market House, in Morrab Gardens and in the Bullock Market, later to become known as the Green Market. Surely its proudest days were those spent in the middle of the old cattle market, that colourful, noisy, bustling hub of local life, where it was much favoured by farmers as a tethering stone for their animals?

King Ricatus may well have been the penultimate Cornish king. The cross probably dates from between AD 900 and 930.

Places of Interest in the Neighbourhood
64. A Punning Device
65. Penzance's Library in a Garden
66. Cornwall's most Bizarre Building in a Street of Curiosities
68. 'The Hoar Rock in the Wood'
69. A Causeway financed by Sinners

68 'The Hoar Rock in the Wood'

Position: St Michael's Mount in Mount's Bay, offshore from Marazion
Ordnance Map: Land's End & The Lizard: Sheet 203 1:50 000
Map Ref: SW/515/298
Access: Accessible across the Causeway from Marazion at low tide, or
by boat from Penzance. St Michael's Mount is now in the care of the
National Trust, and there is a landing fee.

Note: St Michael's Mount, which so pleasingly dominates Mount's Bay
was known in early times as *Carrek Luz en Couze*, or 'The Hoar Rock
In The Wood'; and indeed, traces of a submarine forest are still visible
at low tide (see No. 69). St Michael's Mount is thought to be the 'island
off Britain called Ictis,' documented by the Sicilian Greek historian
Diodorus in the early part of the first century AD, as exporting tin to
the Mediterranean countries before the time of Christ. This place, with
its mystical aura is also associated with the colourful legend that Jesus
came to Cornwall with his tin trading uncle Joseph of Arimathea,
(recalling Blake's 'And did those feet in ancient time, walk upon
England's mountains green?')

It is not surprising that this rocky islet, rising above the waters of
Mount's Bay should have assumed religious importance. It is said,
somewhat fancifully perhaps, that the Phoenicians worshipped Apollo
here, attracting pilgrims who brought offerings. Edward the Confessor
gave the Mount to the monks of St Michael in Normandy, who founded
a priory here. It came into the possession of a succession of notable
families, and has remained with the St Aubyns since 1660.

Places of Interest in the Neighbourhood
64. A Punning Device
65. Penzance's Library in a Garden
66. Cornwall's most Bizarre Building in a Street of Curiosities
67. At the End of its Tether
69. A Causeway financed by Sinners

69 A Causeway financed by Sinners

Position: Marazion Causeway, opposite St Michael's Mount
Ordnance Map: Land's End & The Lizard: Sheet 203 1:50 000
Map Ref: SW/516/306

Note: The two small settlements anciently known as *Marghasbigan* and *Marghasyou* (Market Jew), on the mainland opposite St Michael's Mount, which merged to become Marazion, capitalised on the tin trade and the religious importance of the Mount, to become an important marketing centre long before the rise of Penzance. Ships beached on the Marazion shores for the loading of metal ores and dispatch of cargoes.

The first Archpriest of St Michael's Mount, William Morton, was responsible for constructing the early stone causeway, assisted by the Bishop of Exeter, who called upon sinners to make financial contributions as a way of easing their consciences. And so this all important causeway, allowing vehicular access to St Michael's Mount at low tide paid its debt in quiet minds.

From time to time various horses, oxen, waggons and their handlers became victims of the rising tide; situations which led to drowning or heroic rescues by local boatmen.

At exceptionally low tide another curiosity is revealed in the form of a submarine forest just offshore between here and Wherrytown, carbon dated by Sir Gavin de Beer at around 1700 BC.

Places of Interest in the Neighbourhood
64. A Punning Device
65. Penzance's Library in a Garden
66. Cornwall's most Bizarre Building in a Street of Curiosities
67. At the End of its Tether
68. 'The Hoar Rock in the Wood'

70 The Mên-an-Tol

Position: A holed stone on the moors, to the north west of Madron.
Ordnance Map: Land's End & The Lizard: Sheet 203 1:50 000
Map Ref: SW/425/349
Access: Take the Morvah road from the village of Madron, then follow
the signed footpath at Bosullow Common, about 3½ miles from
Madron.

Note: The Mên-an-Tol ('stone of the hole') is an impressive circular
granite slab, about 4 feet across and one foot thick, with a neatly etched
hole about 20 inches in diameter, which resembles a granite millstone
standing on edge. No one can be really certain as to the origins of this
stone, but theories abound. Originally it may well have served as a
porthole stone, allowing restricted access to some burial vault. The
bardic priesthood attached significance to it, and it has long been
regarded, together with the two phallic looking longstones nearby, as a
symbol of fertility. This stone, locally referred to as the Crick Stone,
was thought to have curative powers. The popular belief was that
anyone suffering from a crick in the back or any other part of the
anatomy would experience relief, after crawling nine times through the
hole in the centre stone, going against the sun's course. For centuries
young children suffering from rickets were brought here, to be passed
naked through the Mên-an-Tol 3 times, then drawn on the grass 3 times
against the sun.

While some subscribed to the superstitious, others favoured the
astronomical. That eminent astronomer, Sir Norman Lockyer, lent his
scientific weight to the theory that the upright stones at either side were
sighting stones for observing the sunrise in May and August, while
looking the other direction in February and March one focused on the
sunset.

Places of Interest in the Neighbourhood
71. The Prehistoric Village
72. A Pirate's Grave?

71 The Prehistoric Village

Position: Chysauster Village 2½ miles to the north of Penzance
[English Heritage]
Ordnance Map: Land's End & The Lizard: Sheet 203 1:50 000
Map Ref: SW/472/350
Access: Approached on B3311 Penzance to St Ives road, turning left at
Badger's Cross

Note: This intriguing prehistoric village consisting of eight beehive
shaped dwellings arranged in pairs on either side of a street was
described by Sir Nikolaus Pevsner as 'the best preserved group of
courtyard houses in the county.' The indications are that timber
uprights fitted into stone sockets supported the apex of the roofs, and
that the houses had paved floors with drains beneath. Small terraces
adjoining the houses suggest prehistoric gardens, while terraces on the
hillside would indicate that the small community supported itself by
mixed farming. The houses are positioned to face east or north east,
thereby avoiding the impact of the prevailing south westerlies. There is
a *fougou* (ruined chamber) nearby.

The rather pleasing name of this ancient village is derived from the
adjacent farm, which, in 1313 was called *Chisalvestre*, which meant
'Silvester's Cottage.'

Places of Interest in the Neighbourhood
70. The Mên-an-Tol
72. A Pirate's Grave?

72 A Pirate's Grave?

Position: In Gulval churchyard, a few yards from the east wall of the church
Ordnance Map: Land's End & The Lizard: Sheet 203 1:50 000
Map Ref: SW/485/318

Note: John Thomas of Marazion, 'who left this life for a better on Sunday 16th day of December 1753, and in y 62d year of his age', also left an intriguing mystery behind him. For his fine and remarkably well preserved horizontal tomb slab bears a striking looking skull and crossbones beneath the inscription 'WANT EXCELL', which has led to the local belief that John of Marazion was a swashbuckling, 18th century pirate. Whether this was the case or not, he was clearly a much loved man, for the rest of the inscription, written along the other three sides advises us:

'If you would live belov'd
and die so . . .'

Also giving him post mortal assurance that:

'We'll studdy to
Imitate you.'

However, the skull and crossbones, a symbol of death, is occasionally seen in Cornish churchyards. Inside the church are memorials to the influential and bountiful Bolitho family.

Places of Interest in the Neighbourhood
70. The Mên-an-Tol
71. The Prehistoric Village

73 Helston's 'Gothic' Archway

Position: At the bottom of Coinagehall Street, Helston
Ordnance Map: Land's End & The Lizard: Sheet 203 1:50 000
Map Ref: SW/654/274

Note: Looking down Coinagehall Street, one gains the full effect of the neo-Gothic archway, erected in 1834 by subscription, as a memorial to Humphry Millet Grylls a member of an influential family which, together with the Glynns family, did much for the town. (There are memorials to both families in the church of St Michael.)

This gateway was designed by London architect George Wightwick and constructed of granite ashlar, with buttresses and four octagonal pinnacles. The adjacent bowling green occupies the former site of Helston Castle, once the home of Edmund, Earl of Cornwall, who reputedly felt more drawn to religion than to politics or fighting, and who once put Cornwall's entire revenue at the disposal of Edward I.

The name Coinagehall Street recalls that Helston was one of the four coinage towns of old stannary Cornwall, where the quality of locally produced tin was tested and assessed for taxation purposes.

Places of Interest in the Neighbourhood
74. Symbol of Wreck and Rescue
75. The Boxer's Birthplace
76. Floodwaters freed by Coins in Leathern Purses

74 Symbol of Wreck and Rescue

Position: Cannon, outside the Folk Museum in Church Street, Helston
Ordnance Map: Land's End & The Lizard: Sheet 203 1:50 000
Map Ref: SW/665/275

Note: The cannon from *HMS Anson*, wrecked at Loe Bar, Porthleven, on 29th December, 1807, and salvaged by naval divers from *HMS Seahawk*, is not only an interesting historical relic, but a poignant symbol of wreck and rescue, which was to have far reaching effects in maritime history. For the harrowing experience of witnessing this wreck, with its tragic and seemingly unnecessary heavy loss of human life so close to the shore, caused Henry Trengrouse to devote the rest of his life to the inventing of a life saving apparatus, which could be operated from the shore in a similar situation.

With amazing singlemindedness, Henry Trengrouse spent years designing a simple coastal rescue device. In June 1816 *The West Briton* reported: 'Mr Trengrouse's contrivance for throwing a line is admirably simple in construction, and not the less easy and successful in execution. The experiment was three times repeated, across the mouth of Porthleven harbour, in the presence of the Mayor of Helston, and several other gentlemen, to all of whom it afforded the utmost satisfaction.'

Trengrouse died in 1854, and there is a large stone memorial to him in the churchyard.

Places of Interest in the Neighbourhood
73. Helston's 'Gothic' Archway
75. The Boxer's Birthplace
76. Floodwaters freed by Coins in Leathern Purses

75 The Boxer's Birthplace

Position: Plaque on the wall of 61 Wendron Street, Helston
Ordnance Map: Land's End & The Lizard: Sheet 203 1:50 000
Map Ref: SW/664/278

Note: Helston enjoys the distinction of being the birthplace of Robert
(Bob) Fitzsimmons, Boxing Champion of the World in 1897, and the
only European to have won three world boxing titles; a satisfying piece
of one upmanship that any town would be pleased to retain,
unchallenged.

A plaque on the wall of 61 Wendron Street, a thatched terraced
cottage, proclaims that this was the birthplace in 1863 of the champion.
He gained the title by beating 'Gentleman' Jim Corbett in the United
States of America. Bob Fitzsimmons is also credited with being the
inventor of the punch to the solar plexus, and this may well be the crux
of the matter. For the story goes that his agitated wife at the ringside
got so excited that she suddenly shouted: 'Hit him in the slats!', thereby
inspiring her husband and helping him gain the coveted world title. His
name is also recalled in the Fitzsimmons Arms in Coinagehall Street.
During his career, he had also held the World Middleweight and Light
Heavyweight titles.

Places of Interest in the Neighbourhood
73. Helston's 'Gothic' Archway
74. Symbol of Wreck and Rescue
76. Floodwaters freed by Coins in Leathern Purses

76 Floodwaters freed by Coins in Leathern Purses

Position: Loe Pool and Loe Bar, to the south of Helston
Ordnance Map: Land's End & The Lizard: Sheet 203 1:50 000
Map Ref: SW/643/243
Access: By footpaths from the B3304 to the south west of Helston,
Penrose and Carminowe; the latter off the Gunwalloe road, turn off
A3083 opposite Culdrose.

Note: The waters of the Cober and others streams around Helston are
dammed by nature to create a beautiful and impressive stretch of water
known as Loe Pool, with the barrier of sand constantly washed up by
the sea taking the name Loe Bar.

   Winter flooding brought its problems, as outlined in this account of
1824: 'When the waters extend so far as to obstruct the workings of the
mills at Helston and Carminowe, the millers apply to the Lord of the
Manor, and presenting him with two leathern purses, each containing
three halfpence, solicit his permission to open the bar: this being
granted, workmen are employed by the Mayor of Helston to cut a
passage through the pebbles: and the opening is no sooner made, than
the whole body of water rushes through the aperture with wonderful
force and impetuosity.' Today there is a sluice gate, and Loe Pool is
owned by the National Trust. The walks here are beautiful and varied.

   Not surprisingly, the place has attracted legends, and is a contender
with Dozmary Pool (see No. 8) for being the place where a hand
emerged from the water to receive King Arthur's sword Excalibur.

Places of Interest in the Neighbourhood
73. Helston's 'Gothic' Archway
74. Symbol of Wreck and Rescue
75. The Boxer's Birthplace

77 A Far Famed Fig Tree

Position: Fig tree in the wall of Manaccan church
Ordnance Map: Truro, Falmouth & surrounding area: Landranger 204
1:50 000
Map Ref: SW/763/249
Access: Look for the signs to Manaccan to the east of the B3293
between Gweek and St Keverne

Note: No one knows how Manaccan's famous fig tree, which grows out
of the south west wall of the church close to the tower, first came to
take root, but it is known to have been there for two hundred years.
The solidly Norman construction, with two stone walls infilled with
rubble, provided suitable conditions for the fig tree to become
established.

In 1893, it was recorded that 'on the south side of the tower is a large
fig tree, growing out of the churchwall, more than a century old, with a
trunk eighteen inches in diameter; its roots penetrate the thickness of
the wall.' It went on to say that during alterations to the church the root
system was found to have penetrated beneath the seats for a
considerable distance. The fig tree has been pruned at various times
since then, but presumably tree and church have developed a means of
mutual support.

Places of Interest in the Neighbourhood
73. Helston's 'Gothic' Archway
74. Symbol of Wreck and Rescue
75. The Boxer's Birthplace
76. Floodwaters freed by Coins in Leathern Purses
78. The Marconi Connection

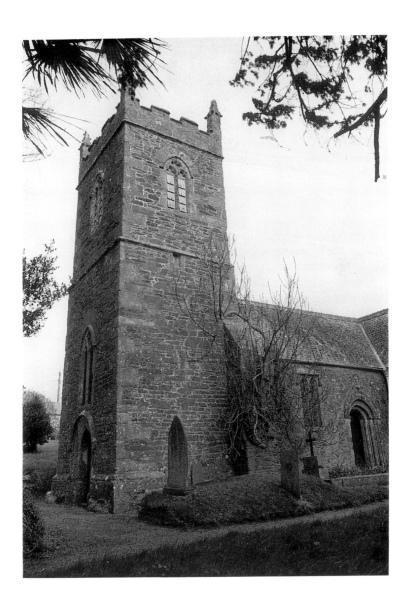

78 The Marconi Connection

Position: The Marconi Monument on Poldhu Point, to the west of Mullion
Ordnance Map: Land's End & The Lizard: Sheet 203 1:50 000
Map Ref: SW/663/196
Access: From the car park at Poldhu Cove, walk up the left hand lane to Poldhu Point

Note: The tall granite monument standing in its exposed clifftop situation at Poldhu, marks the former site of the Marconi Wireless Telegraphy Station, from which Marconi transmitted the first wireless signal across the Atlantic on 12 December 1901. Until it was pulled down in 1937, this impressive Radio Station with its four large towers and steel masts was a dominating landmark for miles.

The tests carried out between here and Sydney on a wave length of 100 metres and a power of about 30 kilowatts in 1924, attracted attention to the possibilities of short wave 'beam' wireless. The invention and development of wireless telegraphy will always be associated with Marconi, who built on the work of earlier pioneers. Guglielmo Marconi, of Italian Irish parentage, was fascinated with the possibilities of electromagnetic radiation and its potential application in the communications field. He came to England in 1896, where his talent was recognised and his work encouraged by Sir William Preece, then Engineer in Chief of the British Post Office. Today the fast moving communications story continues at Goonhilly Down only 2½ miles from Poldhu, where Britain's first satellite earth station was established in 1962 (see No. 80).

Places of Interest in the Neighbourhood
76. Floodwaters freed by Coins in Leathern Purses
77. A Far Famed Fig Tree
79. The Lighthouse on the Lizard
80. Situated in Antiquity and Reaching for the Skies

79 The Lighthouse on the Lizard

Position: The Lizard Lighthouse on Lizard Point
Ordnance Map: Land's End & The Lizard: Sheet 203 1:50 000
Map Ref: SW/705/116

Note: The distinctive twin towers of the Lizard Lighthouse, marking mainland Britain's most southerly point, serve to remind us that this was the site of Cornwall's first real lighthouse in 1619. Previous attempts to light up the Cornish coast for mariners had been made by local charitable and religious initiatives, but they had proved ineffectual. Sir John Killigrew, of the family responsible for the rise of Falmouth (See No. 43), applied for a patent, and agreed to erect a lighthouse here at his own expense, with the promise that the light should be extinguished at the approach of the enemy.

Sir John hoped to meet the cost of maintenance with contributions from owners of passing ships, but with little success. In the face of opposition from Trinity House, James I set a fee of one halfpenny a ton on all vessels passing the light. This unpopular move resulted in the patent being withdrawn, the light extinguished and the tower demolished. Clearly, the Lizard needed another lighthouse, but it was not until 1748 that Trinity House granted permission for Thomas Fonnereau to erect a replacement. It had two towers and an observation cottage between, from which an overlooker, reclining on a couch, could keep an eye on the brightness of the coal fired lanterns, and give a salutary blast on the cowhorn as a subtle hint to get busy on the bellows if they dimmed. Oil lights were eventually installed, as was a fog signal. In 1874 *The West Briton* announced that 'the electric light will replace the Argand lamps, which have been in use from the beginning of the century.' These beautiful reflectors are still in use, with small indentations giving clues to hot oil drippings of long ago.

Today the Lizard Lighthouse is a highly sophisticated nerve centre for all the unmanned lighthouses in West Cornwall.

Places of Interest in the Neighbourhood
77. A Far Famed Fig Tree
78. The Marconi Connection
80. Situated in Antiquity and Reaching for the Skies

80 Situated in Antiquity and Reaching for the Skies

Position: Goonhilly Satellite Earth Station, Goonhilly Downs, near Helston
Ordnance Map: Truro, Falmouth & surrounding area Sheet 204 1:50 000
Map Ref: SW/728/213
Access: (Open for visiting between Easter and the end of September) Goonhilly Satellite Earth Station on Goonhilly Downs, 7 miles from Helston on the B3293, St Keverne road, on the right.

Note: The awe inspiring futuristic cluster of TV dishes projecting heavenwards on Goonhilly Downs, amidst the standing stones, hut circles and tumuli left by our early ancestors, combines the mystery of the distant past, our responsibility for the present and the wonder of the future, where earth knows no bounds.

By virtue of its geographical situation, Cornwall has long played an important role in the evolving story of communications (see No. 78). In 1962 the National Aeronautical & Space Administration of the United States of America launched the experimental Telstar 1, demonstrating the potential of global television and telecommunication. At that time three large capacity Earth Stations in France, the United States and here were ready to exchange signals through the new device. Goonhilly Satellite Earth Station was designed and built in only twelve months, and it has developed considerably since. This is a modern curiosity, in which visitors can tune into Global TV, search out the heavens, watch pictures and events beamed across the sky and be part of the action of the exciting technology of the 21st century.

Places of Interest in the Neighbourhood
77. A Far Famed Fig Tree
78. The Marconi Connection
79. The Lighthouse on the Lizard

Index